FRESH LOOKS
AT
DEER HUNTING

OTHER RECENT BOOKS BY BYRON W. DALRYMPLE

BYRON DALRYMPLE ON TROUT FISHING

DOVES AND DOVE SHOOTING

COMPLETE GUIDE TO GAME FISH

FRESH LOOKS
AT
DEER HUNTING

By Byron W. Dalrymple

Printing Code
    11, 12, 13, 14, 15

        Library of Congress Cataloging-in-Publication Data

Dalrymple, Byron W., 1914-
    Fresh looks at deer hunting / by Byron Dalrumple.
        p.   cm.
    ISBN 0-8329-0471-6 : $24.95
    1. Deer hunting.   I. Title.
    SK301.D355   1992
    799.2'77357—dc20
                                                    92-31258
                                                    CIP

To Ellen

for reasons enough to fill
several books this size

CONTENTS

ACKNOWLEDGMENTS

Author and publisher express their thanks and gratitude to publications listed below for their permission to reprint articles by Byron W. Dalrymple. Some of these were published originally in somewhat different form.

"How Much Do Deer Really Weigh?" — *Field & Stream* — July 1985

"Freak Deer Antlers" — *Field & Steam* — October 1983

"Essence of Deer" — *Field & Stream* — September 1987

"To Find A Deer, Know What You're Looking For" — *American Hunter* — September 1978

"Successful Whitetail Hunting" — *Field & Stream* — December 1977

"Zero In On Deer" — *Field & Stream* — September 1982

"Living With Whitetails" — *Field & Stream* — June 1986

"Whitetail Body Language" — *American Hunter* — November 1975

"The Mulie Personality" — *Field & Stream* — November 1982

"Calling Deer" — *Field & Stream* — April 1984

"The Rut" — *Field & Stream* — October 1980

"Rattle Up a Buck" — *American Hunter* — March 1977

"The Sportiest Way for Whitetails" — *Field & Stream* — April 1987

"The Luck Of The Draw" — *Field & Stream* — September 1983

"Be Ready When The Deer Is" — *Field & Stream* — May 1987

"The Midday Deer Hunter" — *Field & Stream* — January 1981

"Guessers, Gamblers & Monsters" — *Field & Stream* — September 1985

"Hunting Western Whitetails" — *Sports Afield Hunting Annual* — 1976

"Exquisite Anguish" — *Field & Stream* — July 1990

"The Miniature Whitetail" — *American Hunter* — March 1981

"The Whitetails You Miss" — *Field & Stream* — December 1978

"Sitting for Deer" — *Field & Stream Deer Guide* — 1984

"Computerize Deer Hunt Plan" — *American Hunter* — February 1978

"Thin Cover Mulies" — *Field & Stream Deer Guide* — 1981

"Whitetails On The Move" — *Field & Stream Deer Guide* — 1984

"Making Sense of Deer Senses" — *Field & Stream Hunting Annual* — 1983

"100-Acre Deer Hunt" — *American Hunter* — June 1982

"Hope For A Storm" — *Field & Stream* — December 1981

"Deer Hunting Malarkey" — *Field & Stream* — February 1982

"West Texas' Double-Barrel Buck Action" — *Texas Fish & Game* — October 1990

"The Making Of A Deer Hunter" — *American Hunter* — March 1979

"Deer! Who Needs 'em?" — *Southern Outdoors — B.A.S.S.* — September 1991

FRESH LOOKS
AT
DEER HUNTING

INTRODUCTION

As both a deer hunter and a so-called senior citizen, I take great delight in flipping through the thick card file of memory, reliving in detail many of the experiences of almost sixty years of observing and hunting deer. Whitetails from Maine to the Great Lakes states to Wyoming to Texas and the South, mule deer down the Rockies from Canada to Mexico. It was the *hunts* that furnished the real drama. Some of the kills were triumphs of a sort, most were only split second climaxes to the thrills of successful plotting.

Several kills during my early years, I'll grant, had their own special satisfaction, those on running deer, before I got the vinegar out of me and understood that these were a poor practice, simply examples of lack of restraint. After that I took pride in refusing to let the deer dictate to me when to shoot. I came to understand that matters to take pride in were turning down shots I found unacceptable, hunting craftily enough so I had the animal standing just so — the way *I* wanted it.

One early-day running shot I'll never forget, however, was a kill that was high drama and a complete surprise, at the great range of fifteen steps. Eager to experiment, I was carrying a 12-gauge shotgun, full choke, with a shell loaded with 00 buckshot — nine big pellets. I wanted to try the buckshot, but I was uneasy about the possible results.

Down to my right a hundred or more yards a companion was walking along the same low ridge I was on. Suddenly I heard a racket, then could distinguish on that still morning the thump of deer hoofs hitting the lightly frozen ground. This forest was of poplar, white birch, maples, and assorted conifers. But there was an open area in front of me. The buck burst from the timber, running all out. I had often hunted ruffed grouse here, and so my natural inclination was to swing the shotgun as if I were tracking a crossing bird. When the barrel was pointing barely in front of the bounding buck's nose, I touched off.

I remember that excitement enveloped me, but as a pretty fair bird shooter, I shot coolly enough, yet was hardly able to believe buckshot could kill a big eight-point whitetail of possibly 175 pounds on the hoof. At the shattering boom of the gun, the deer folded, dropped, skidded several feet on the leaf covered turf. I stood there astonished. Admittedly that kill was high drama. It was also the only time I ever tried buckshot.

I relate the incident to emphasize that deer have always so intrigued me that I wanted to try every hunting method, and to watch them at every opportunity. As an inveterate trout fisherman, I often paused on streams scattered across the nation to watch the actions and reactions of whitetails or mule deer as they spotted me. I've sat in photo blinds and hunting blinds hour after hour observing deer, their social life, their body language. For years now on our own rugged ranch in the Texas Hill Country I've spent more time watching at all seasons than hunting. And on our home place in the country, where we have a modest, wooded acreage and two ponds, I've even been able to look up from my work and observe deer almost any day of the year, testing to see what signs and sounds disturbed them, which forbs they ate, and the interaction of groups.

What all this and my wide hunting experience led me to conclude long ago is that the bulk of popular literature, in both magazines and books — millions of words of it over the years — is too shallow and repetitive. In my long writing career, with scores of magazine pieces about deer and hunting for them, I've tried constantly to probe deeper than the usual, to take fresh looks. A collection of those is presented here.

Abundant and well managed as deer herds are today, it's true that the rankest tyro can go into the woods carrying in his head only the oft repeated rudiments, and put venison on the table. However, the real challenges and satisfactions come to those who glean deeper knowledge, by closer study of their targets. Then the hunt, deftly performed, is the prideful, gratifying part. The kill is only the momentary conclusion of a carefully crafted plan based on intimate, detailed knowledge of the quarry.

Buck follows track of another deer. Gland betweeen the toes exudes waxy substance that leaves scent in tracks.

The malformed antlers of this big mule deer, collected by the author in far western Texas, make an unusual trophy.

CHAPTER 1

LEARNING ABOUT DEER WEIGHTS, FREAK ANTLERS, AND SCENT GLANDS

An old rule regarding deer weight states: a buck viewed before the shot doubles in size, loses one-half when first seen at close range aground, gains it back while being dragged out, adds another half while being hung up.

A friend who'd recently bagged his first whitetail told me, "When I was field dressing it I knew I'd popped a real buster. I guessed its weight, gutted, at 175 pounds. By the time my partner and I had dragged it out, we agreed I'd underestimated. This buck would easily go 250. When it was weighed at the locker, I was inclined to disbelieve the scale. It read 110!"

Deer hunters are notoriously poor judges of what their kills weigh. Wistful exaggeration when guessing weight is endemic among hunters. Mature bucks look big. They also feel big when you try to move them or hang them up. Most, however, shrink substantially when actually weighed.

One factor especially confuses the issue of what deer really weigh. State to state, even county to county, deer size may differ drastically because of habitat differences. Where I live, mature whitetail bucks field dress at 70 or 80 pounds. Move to fringes of my region, and they'll dress out at 100 to 115 pounds. Go south 100 miles and field-dressed mature bucks weigh in at 150 to 175 pounds. The biggest buck I've killed there dressed out at 188 pounds. Using the standard recommended by many biologists — 25 percent weight loss from field dressing — that deer on the hoof was an authentic 250-pounder.

General belief is that mule deer weigh much more than whitetails. They are somewhat heavier, but field-dressed 300-pounders aren't as common as many tall tales would have you believe. In a weighed sample of 360 Rocky Mountain mule deer a few years ago, less than 1 percent weighed 300 pounds. However, deer of both varieties do occasionally weigh that much. Maine is renowned for a few whitetails each season that field dress in the 300-pound category. The Great Lakes region and the Midwest also turn up occasional bruisers. In 1962, an Iowa hunter bagged a 440-pound deer. Wisconsin authorities some years ago recorded two deer weighing 481 and 491 pounds. Several decades ago, Minnesota recorded an astounding whitetail of 511 pounds. Freaks? Probably.

A check of several authoritative references by recognized deer experts shows they closely agree on what average live mature bucks weigh, nationwide. While noting that whitetails may vary regionally from 75 to 300 pounds, the standard all give averages around 150 pounds, with general variations from 125 to 165 pounds. Mule deer standards are 145 to 175 pounds, with a substantial number running 200 to 220 pounds, occasional deer to 300 pounds, and a rare few between 400 and 450 pounds. All agree that on-the-hoof mature blacktail bucks average 150 pounds or less. Rarely does a blacktail buck weigh 175 pounds, and very rarely does one weigh up to 300 pounds. Deduct 25 percent from any of these live weights, and you'll have a measure of general field-dressed results.

A vastly experienced deer hunting friend who kept records of field-dressed weights of deer he shot told me: "Of seventy mature whitetail bucks, taken from Maine to the Great Lakes to the Deep South to Texas, the majority weighed in the 100- to 140-pound range. Only a few weighed 150 pounds and over. Of thirty-two mule deer, taken from Montana to Arizona, a surprising number were no heavier than the whitetails, ranging from 115 to 135 pounds. Several weighed around 150 pounds, one weighed 170 pounds, and another weighed 186 pounds. The largest, killed near Arvada, Wyoming, weighed 235 pounds."

A massive statistical deer study compiled by Sidney Wilcox, a professor at Arizona State University, annually gathered material from biologists in all fifty states over a seven-year period. Among the figures were field-dressed yearly weight averages of each state's total deer kill. These of course include all age groups. The figures are intriguing and dampen the brags of hunters about how much "almost any little old deer" from their area weighs.

For example, whitetail weights re-averaged by region, all states of each area used, show the following: South and Southeast, 98 pounds; Great Lakes, 120 pounds; Northeast, 115 pounds; Central and Midwest, 118 pounds; West, 108 pounds. The average for the whole U.S., which reflects the field-dressed weights of millions of deer, was 112 pounds. The mule deer average of all Western states was 126 pounds. The blacktail deer average was 102 pounds.

For many hunters there will be two surprises here: that whitetail weights average out region-to-region with such a modest variation; and that the average field-dressed weights of all deer are so low. Not so surprising, I suspect, is that numerous hunters reading these statistics will be heard to mutter, "Well, *my* deer was bigger — even if I did guess at it!"

FREAK ANTLERS

Every season deer hunters hear about, or see, or tag, bucks with freak antlers. Perhaps one antler is high and normal, the other short and deformed. Both may be knurled nubs, one may have a dropped tine, or there may be a drooped whole antler on one side. Occasionally antlers are hard, but still clothed in stiff, spiny velvet. The non-typical classes in the Boone & Crockett records are actually freak heads.

Such antlers elicit high interest. Quite a lot is known about what causes them, but since few hunters really understand how they come about, many tall tales circulate. Although there are several known causes, the effect of bodily injury is one of the most intriguing.

A classic example concerns a whitetail buck we spotted one fall on our place in Texas. At first sighting, all we could see was the right antler — tall, symmetrical with five points and of trophy proportions. When the buck turned its head, however, trophy illusions vanished. The left antler was a short, crumpled deformity. When the buck ran, we saw that it was missing its right hind leg from above the knee joint. We saw that buck for two seasons. Antler growth pattern was the same: normal right, crumpled left. Biological studies, I discovered, have shown that a high percentage of buck deer injured in a hind leg — broken bones, wounds, injured tendons — develop a deformed antler on the opposite side, which may occur from year to year.

Curiously, injured forelegs or shoulders usually produce an opposite pattern. A friend last year collected a freak mule deer that limped badly in its left foreleg. When skinned, the left shoulder blade showed evidence of having been broken and healed. The left antler was a twisted spike curving down behind the left ear. The right was normal. Studies suggest that foreleg injuries produce freak antler growth on the *same* side.

Disease — brain tumors, for example — sometimes results in freak antlers. Poor diet is a common cause of deformities. On a park tract in Kentucky where no hunting was allowed, deer became so abundant they destroyed their habitat almost to the starvation point. It was noted that the bucks grew antlers which never hardened. In numerous counties of the Edwards Plateau in Texas, deer are so overpopulous and compete so severely with angora goats for their forage that a high percentage produce small, deformed freak antlers.

One ten-year study of fenced-in whitetail bucks found that the incidence of freak and exceptional antlers were both genetically related. A buck with no injuries but with freak antlers several years running often produced buck progeny with malformed antlers. Of course many freaks result from antler injuries while the antlers are soft and in velvet. I've often watched bucks in velvet on our ranch and observed how careful they are not to strike their antlers on branches. They're very tender then. Most injuries at that time show on hardened antlers as a knob, a bulb at the end of a tine, or a beam ending in a stub.

Most curious of all are the so-called "cactus" bucks. These bucks have antlers that are hard, but still have most or some of the velvet in place. It shows as short, stiff hairlike growth. The mule deer antlers on my office wall appear as a pair of grossly malformed club-like beams — each roughly 18 inches long and about 5 inches around throughout their length. There are knobs and short points at the bases, and stiff velvet covers much of the antlers. The buck was burly and vigorous, and had probably carried those antlers for several seasons.

"Cactus" bucks usually do not shed antlers. The growth is due to a malfunction of the gonads, which may have been caused by an injury. However, studies of nontypical recordbook entries for both whitetails and mule deer, plus other deer studies from several states, show an interesting fact — an inordinate number of cactus bucks with perfectly normal appearance, but with nonfunctional gonads come from specific areas. Although scientists aren't positive why this occurs, it has been established that invariably the region's soil is a coarse and infertile granitic mixture of quartz and mica. A relationship between the freak antlers and this soil type (and its resulting vegetation) is suspected.

SCENT GLANDS

Deer hunters nowadays use scents as standard hunting equipment. Some of these mask hunter odors. Others supposedly attract deer, and there is substantial evidence that occasionally these scents actually do the job. Few hunters, however, know much about how deer use scents of their own, and how important these are in the animals' social lives, during the rut, in marking trails, helping them find their way, announcing their presence to other deer, warning of danger, or indicating fear. Hunters can use this knowledge to their own advantage.

The senses of deer have been carefully studied. Although hearing and sight are keen, scientists point out that the sense of smell is the keenest sense deer possess. There's a logical probable reason for this. In often dense cover, deer can't and don't see each other or properly identify possible danger by sight over long distances. They may listen to each other moving about at close range, but they seldom com-

municate vocally. In a lifetime of deer hunting and watching, I've rarely heard deer produce vocal sounds, and most hunters would agree.

I've heard a fawn caught by dogs scream much the same as a young
domestic goat in similar anguish. A doe caught in a fence may blat
as she struggles. Strayed fawns occasionally bleat softly and mothers
may reply. Several times I've heard a rutting buck following a doe in
heat utter a series of low, gutteral grunts. However, vocal utterances
are uncommon. Most deer communication depends upon odors the
animals produce.

These are chiefly from secretions of paired skin glands. Among
the most important of these to the daily life of deer are the interdigital
— between the toes — glands. These are present on all four feet. Many
hunters aren't even aware of these glands and what they do. Each is
a fold of tissue forming a sac that produces a yellowish, waxy substance.
Openings are located along each hoof section. At every step, the odor
of the secretion is deposited.

If you get a close-range whiff, you'll find this odor extremely un-
pleasant. Interestingly, I discovered by examining the interdigital glands
of several whitetails and several mule deer that they're much larger
on the former. Biologists have suggested that whitetails, which dwell
in cover, require more scent secretion than mule deer, which are able
to see each other more readily on open slopes and also are more
gregarious.

Here's an illustration of how important trail scents can be. A
rancher friend of mine has a permit to keep whitetails in a pen. He
occasionally releases them. They roam widely, but because they're quite
tame they come back toward evening to be fed. One day he graded
a ranch road after he'd turned them out and they'd crossed it.

"When they returned," he told me, "they milled around by the road,
confused. I suspected it was because I'd wiped out their scented trail.
Sure enough, when I repeated the routine, the same thing occurred."

There's a lesson here for hunters about scented deer trails. Study
the feet of deer you've shot, and you'll discover that there's no way
the animals can take a step without leaving scent from one foot or
another. This strengthens the indication that trail marking by the inter-
digitals is extremely important. I've watched a doe trail her own half-
grown fawn that had wandered away. Many hunters have seen bucks
put their nose to the ground to trail a doe during rut. He may be using
several of her scents, but where numerous deer tracks are cluttered

on a trail, a buck unerringly puts its nose close to the ground to pick out the one he's following.

The most noticeable glands on deer are the metatarsal glands, located low on the outside shank of each hind leg. These are horny ridges bordered by stiff hair. Size and shape differ among deer species and some subspecies — so much so, in fact, that the metatarsal alone can be used to identify deer species: whitetail, short, about 2 inches, pear shaped; mule deer, up to 5 inches long, narrowly elliptical; Columbian blacktail, slightly over half the size as on mule deer. These glands exude an oily, odorous substance. Some biologists believe fright triggers metatarsal secretions. To date, research hasn't substantiated this, nor precisely how the metatarsals relate to deer communication. Scientists note that, curiously, small metatarsals are found on the less gregarious whitetails, larger ones on the more social mule deer.

The paired scent glands with which hunters are most familiar are the tarsals, located inside each hind leg at the hock. The tufts of long hair surrounding these glands easily mark them. Few realize how many uses musk from these glands has. Whenever a deer is fearful and suspicious, or shows evidence of hostility toward another deer, the tufts of hair surrounding the tarsal glands are elevated. At these times there may be no musk visible on the hair. But the glands are visibly wet and also smelly during the rut.

Endless arguments ensue among hunters over whether or not the tarsals should be removed before field dressing or skinning. The musk cannot get into the meat on its own. But if you inadvertently get it on your hands and then handle the meat, it may be offensively tainted. If you are skeptical about the power of this musk, get some on your hands on purpose, and then try to wash it off. You'll be smelling it a week later! As a precaution when field dressing, I remove the tarsals, along with a wide swatch of surrounding hide.

All deer, even small fawns, try to urinate on the tarsal tufts, pressing their hocks together to accomplish it. This combination musk and urine scent is used year-round. Does use it to locate fawns that have strayed. Fawns use it to locate their mothers. Does also warn fawns by discharging tarsal musk, which can be done at will. There may be different strengths of the scent for different purposes.

The most abundant use of tarsal musk is during breeding season. Bucks make scrapes and urinate on their hocks and thus wet the scrape with this mixture. Does visit scrapes and do likewise, advising the buck of their availability. As they move about during the rut, both sexes leave the scent on trailside bushes and in the air along their routes. Although little known to hunters, sudden tarsal discharge in any season by a spooked deer warns and puts others to flight. These glands thus serve as a prime source of year-round scent communication.

Another pair of scent glands, the preorbitals, are at the corners of the eyes. For unknown reasons, these are much larger on mule deer than on whitetails. Part of the purpose of these glands is to lubricate and clean the eyes. But recent research suggests more complex uses. Does angry at other does have been observed flaring these glands as they strike out with their forefeet. Although the secretion of these glands is not as odorous as that from the others, observers believe it is used by bucks to mark twigs or limbs above scrapes during the rut.

On numerous occasions I've watched a buck make a scrape, always with a limb overhanging it within reach. The animal then reaches high, nuzzles and nibbles at leaves or twigs, and hooks at the limb with its antlers. Close observation shows that during this activity the twigs or leaves are passed across the preorbitals. Numerous observations of this behavior led scientists long ago to conclude that the preorbital secretion is used as a marker. Some believe it is also deposited for the same purpose on twigs along trails as a buck marks off his territory.

More intriguing, recent research suggests that when a buck makes a rub on a sapling, it's not all for the purposes — as was once thought — of cleaning off velvet and polishing antlers. Preorbital secretion is deposited on the rub. Suspicion has grown that this secretion may not be as important during breeding season as another from the skin of the forehead. As a buck rubs and strips bark from the sapling, the forehead is vigorously employed in a kind of mock goring action. The buck, it is thought, thus leaves a scent marker of his specific identity. Studies of deer scalps before and during rut tend to indicate some glandular activity.

Without question, each buck has an individual standing in the deer community of a given territory and leaves individual scent markers proclaiming his dominant — or submissive — status. On two occasions while on stand, I have watched whitetail bucks examine and sniff a rub and a limb above a scrape that I knew had been made by a "boss buck" of the territory. In one instance the deer was a young forkhorn. In the other it was a mature, husky, heavy-antlered six-pointer. On each occasion the bucks appeared nervous and sneaked off. They seemed to know from the scent that this was no buck with which to tangle.

Hunters who've had the opportunity to watch undisturbed deer know that at any season they routinely identify each other by sniffing. Does identify which fawn is theirs by scent. One doe sniffs another and decides to give her a swipe with a front hoof. A strange deer wanders in, is given the scent test, and is promptly run off or accepted. Remarkably, when one or several deer have been startled and have fled, another that wanders into the area right afterward often becomes suddenly alert, suspicious, sniffs the air, and decides to leave. Certainly much is still to be learned about deer communication via their odors. However, hunters who properly interpret what's already known can apply the knowledge to enhance their hunting success.

Too many hunters imagine they'll see a whole buck, close range, spang in the open. That's unlikely.

Whitetail buck in deep shadow in woods. You have to look sharp to find such deer, or to see some part of a deer.

CHAPTER 2

TO FIND A DEER —
KNOW WHAT YOU'RE LOOKING FOR

Mule deer buck in low brush, photographed on overcast day with telephoto lens equal to 8X binocular. The unaided eye probably would miss this deer.

In the mind's eye of many hunters, a deer is a great big critter that should loom like a horse on the horizon. In reality, however, the average deer, whitetail or mule deer, is not a very large animal after all when actually measured. But who knows the measurements of deer? Very few hunters, that's sure.

A couple of seasons back I got stuck to help out as a guide for an afternoon on a large ranch in western Texas. Here dwell desert mule deer in substantial numbers. The gentleman I was to go out with was on his first mule deer hunt, and we were not half a mile down the road in my four-wheel-drive when I began to suspect he was looking for something that didn't exist — a mule deer probably three or four times as big as whitetails and maybe 10 feet tall.

There was a lot of brush along the foothills. Finally, I stopped and meticulously glassed a sweep of it. I found a buck — part of one — at 75 yards that I hated to let him pass up. All I could see were curved antler tips and indistinct points, and lower down antler bases, and some neck. An ample amount of neck for a shot. The distance between the antler tips, and the size of the bases, easily identified this as a fine buck, even though I couldn't precisely count points. But I could see brow tines at the bases, and enough tips to know this was, full count, either an eight or 10.

The deer felt it was hidden and I wasn't too worried that it would quickly run off. Trying to speak calmly so not to shake the man up, I told him what I was looking at and tried patiently to get him a fix on it. It was no use. He had the right place, a big Spanish bayonet on either side of the brush where the deer stood.

Finally he blurted in exasperation, "I simply can't see any buck's head sticking out of that brush, or his back."

It now dawned on me what he was looking for — not a piece of a deer *in* the brush but sticking way up above it. About then the buck had enough. It bolted. It was a beauty. Before the hunter could take up the slack in his jaw the deer was 500 yards away.

I had him get out, without his rifle. I got out. "I'm going to walk into this brush," I told him. "I'm five feet seven. I want you to see how tall this brush is around here."

It proved to be six inches to a foot above my head. That really isn't very tall cover. Further, with mountains looming behind, this was a new perspective for the hunter. He just couldn't believe the brush would cover me. Then I gave him some mule deer measurements, and this was harder yet for him to accept. It takes a big mule deer to stand 40 inches at the shoulder. A few may go to 42. More likely average ones will be about 36 to 38.

Now then, a hunter of average build, with boots on, will measure about 36 inches at his hip joint, and 40 to 42 at his belt line. In other words, if you stood beside a big buck mule deer, the top of its back would be at your belt line. That may seem astonishing, but it is true. If the buck has its head erect — it doesn't hold its head fully erect, but on a forward angle — the top of its skull will be on the average no more than 12 inches higher than the back line. This means that on this same average-build hunter of five feet seven inches height the top of the buck's head will be at least four inches *below his chin*.

Antlers, of course, differ in configuration. Tall ones on mule deer seldom reach a height of much over 15 to 16 inches. Thus the highest antler tips on a truly stunning buster of a mulie buck won't reach more than three inches above this average hunter's head. This, mind you, is a *big* buck. Scale it down to average, say 38 inches at the shoulder, with smaller antlers, or wider ones. This deer you could swing a leg over as if it were a small pony. Its antler tips, head erect, will be lower than your head.

Now back down to the whitetail. Again, granted, sizes differ widely with locale. The largest bucks will be almost as tall at the shoulder as the mule deer buck, a maximum of about 40 inches. But many small whitetails stand no more than 30 inches at the shoulder, and 36 is a big one. Consider the startling fact that the 30-incher will have shoulder height and back line no higher than the measurements of your inseam! Whitetail antler configuration is usually lower than that of mule deer. Therefore, a big whitetail, 36 inches at shoulder will stand, head erect, with antler tips on the average about five feet.

The chief value of knowing these measurements is so that you can compare them to your own height, and thereby to the cover in which you hunt, or into which you are looking. Don't be deceived by perspective. In the mountains, long vistas change it, confusing a hunter. Brush may look low — but measure it on yourself and then figure how to look for a deer; that is, whether or not you can see a deer above it.

Now consider distance. Here is an animal, considering both species, that stands 2½ to 3½ feet high at the shoulder. At 30 paces it probably looks bigger than that because a hunter sees it both for the size it really is and for the size his imagination and excitement tell him it is. But now move this target out to 100 yards — then 200 — then 300. Imagine looking with your naked eye. Or go out sometime and look at deer-sized objects at these paced distances.

It is amazing how many hunters look for deer on a slope, or across a meadow at the edge of a woods, and in their mind's eye are seeking a deer of full size — that is, full deer size close-up. This is why, even when glassing, numerous hunters are inept. They don't really know what it is they are looking for. A deer facing you, or rear end on, or lying down at various distances offers that much less area to your eye or glass. Learning to keep size in perspective in relation to distance is immensely important.

Sometimes it pays also not to keep looking too far. It has often amused me to hunt with someone, especially in mule deer country, who was searching way off yonder on a mountain where he couldn't hit a deer if he saw one, and could hardly see one because the distance was so great — and here under our noses, within the first 100 yards, every now and then there was a deer partially hidden. The hunter, confusing perspective because distances were so vast they were in a way dwarfed, was looking right over the tops of the deer within range. Habitually looking too close — 25 or 30 yards — is as bad. Few deer are going to be that foolish.

Light, of course, plays an important part in what to look for. It is a fact that a big buck in early slanted bright sun does often look "as big as a horse" way off at 300 yards or more. These are the easy ones to find. They literally shine, and level, bright light tends to light them so brilliantly that they look almost blown up in proportions. On an overcast day, however, a deer in fall coat against most of the backgrounds hunting season offers — even with snow in mixed hardwood and evergreen forest — blends so perfectly it is easy even for the well-schooled "looker" to pass over it. On those days the smart hunter hunts at snail's pace and glasses incessantly and with utmost patience. He also shortens his scanning distance. Deer know they are not easily seen in flat light and may sit tight.

Ultra-low light also changes how a deer looks. If there is no sun at all, I would personally keep looking then for horizontal lines, in perspective once again, against the vertical lines of most cover, i.e. trees, shrubs. The average length of whitetails overall, the way you'd view one broadside, is five to six feet. Mule deer are a bit longer, 5½ to 6½. A horizontal line that long, at the proper height above ground — again in distance perspective — is quite noticeable to the eye of the sharp hunter in or against most kinds of cover.

Many writings have instructed deer hunters never to look for a "whole deer" but for a part of one. Well, that idea is sound but needs qualification. Deer feed most actively during the first two and last two hours of daylight — when they feed in daylight, which they don't do some days. When deer feed, both whitetails and mule deer obviously are on their feet and moving, and either in the open or along the edges. Thus it is a good idea during those hours in particular to actually keep looking for a *whole* deer, while still alert for parts of one.

Obviously much will depend on the *type* of cover. If a deer is browsing along in a patch of brush, naturally you aren't going to see it all at a glance. Nonetheless, these early and late hours are the times when looking for a whole deer is logical. If I were hunting mule deer on the open slopes and mountain meadows where they love to forage, and I had to look distantly, I would think first in terms of whitish or pale color blobs. The rear end of a mule deer, even seen from the side, shows up plainly at great range. Mule deer also are exceedingly gregarious. Thus several pale spots far off on a slope are a dead giveaway — especially if they move, or are seen one moment and not the next.

Of course, when you see the white rear end of a whitetail, it has its tail up and is long gone. But whitetails that are partially hidden and looking toward you show even in weak light the distinct white area under the chin and the upper throat. The spot shows often even from the side. A small white patch among dead weeds, grass, or bushes is not a normal item. The rule is, anything that shouldn't be there may be a deer. Check it.

When my two boys were learning to deer hunt, I always impressed on them that deer antlers, regardless of endless nonsense written or bandied by word of mouth to the contrary, do *not* resemble brush. The beam of an antler has a curve and a look about it that a crisscross of brush does not have. How the view is interpreted depends on how astute an observer you are.

"Look for a part of an antler," I explained to them. "Almost without fail a bit of give-away curve will show. If the deer is standing you can tell by how high up the bit of antler is. If it is broadside, or you suspect it is, then look for the long, horizontal back line, perhaps mostly, but not all, lost in the pattern of cover. Look also for two straight sticks or four properly spaced, coming up out of the ground — legs. Maybe just a hint shows. But if you search for these clues, they may turn into deer."

An old rancher who has never hunted in snow country taught me some years back about contrasts, and of course it is just as important in snow. He told me, "Always keep watch when hunting for spots where a deep shadow among trees, for instance, is backed up behind by sun on grass." Or just the small sunny spot among trees. A deer that moves into shadow with the sun behind is instantly silhouetted.

The art of seeing deer is indeed an endless and intriguing subject. Hopefully, the hints given thus far will help you find deer. But what then? How are you going to know, having found one, whether it is the one you want? A lot of hunters shoot the first deer they get a crack at. If it's legal, and the hunter amenable, that's fine. If one is doe hunting, and the animal is suitable as to size and in good physical shape, the choice of which doe to shoot matters little.

Buck hunting is different. The hunter after a buck — even almost any fair buck — still should know something about judging deer from a distance. Is it or isn't it a buck, in cases where antlers may not show plainly? Not infallibly, but nearly always, a hunter who goes by what I call the triangle and rectangle method can come pretty close. A doe looked at head on makes a distinct triangle from forefeet to shoulders. That is, she usually stands with feet slightly apart for good balance, but her shoulders are narrow, or compressed. Conversely, the shoulders of a buck are broader and the forelegs come up almost straight to meet them.

Looked at broadside, it's even easier. Here again, a doe looks in general body outline, exclusive of head and neck and legs, like a lying-down triangle, the apex toward the front. A broadside buck is blocky, and makes the general outline of a rectangle, with the long dimension being his back and belly lines forming the outline.

Judging antlers is another matter, and involves once again physical measurements for comparison. One fall in a mule deer camp in Texas, guide Jim Barbee and a group of his hunters were eating a big noonday meal at the camp table during which someone brought up the size of a mule deer's ears. Several of the hunters were from out of state, from whitetails-only country.

One who had just killed a good buck and was keyed up over it said, "I couldn't believe the huge size of the ears on that buck."

I couldn't resist asking how long he figured they were, and this got a lively conversation going. Somebody wanted to bet that each ear was at least 15 inches long. A pot was in the making but I didn't have the heart to push it because I knew the answer. It was money too easy to take.

I said, "Tell you what. I could collect your money, but let's do it like this. Somebody go out and measure the ears of every buck that's hung up, and I'll pay two dollars for every one that doesn't measure 11 inches."

What was interesting was that a couple of old hands at mule deer hunting were there, and they thought they were going to pick up a little change. They were very much surprised to find out that 11 inches it was.

Whitetail ears are at least two inches shorter — each ear — and maybe more than that, depending on the race of deer and the locale. Deer do not hold their ears straight out. Especially when alert and looking, they hold them cocked. Without getting involved in complicated formulas and the angle at which a deer holds its ears under varying influences, suffice to say that ear tip to ear tip on a whitetail will be roughly 12 to 14 inches. Mule deer hold their ears somewhat straighter out, even when alert, and their skull is a bit wider. Thus, adding on two inches for each ear, even a conservative mule deer ear measurement will come out at least 18 inches from tip to tip.

Conclude that if you look head on at a whitetail buck and can see antlers curving two inches out beyond each ear, you can make a snap estimate that this buck has a spread of 16 to 18 inches. If the curve is four inches on each side beyond the ears, you better not stand around. A mule deer looked at the same way can be guessed at 22 to 26 inches in spread — and so on.

Few hunters wish to take a straight going-away shot at a deer unless it is a buster they simply have to try for. A quick way to judge is as follows: a straight-away whitetail that shows four inches of antler curve protruding past each of its sides or rump, is a real trophy, 22 to 24 inches in spread, for the body of the deer will be 14 to 16 inches thick; a mule deer is broader in the beam by about three to four inches, thus with four inches of antler showing on each side past the rump it would be 25 to 26 inches in spread.

Always bear in mind that mule deer antlers in particular always seem to look deceptively big, perhaps partly because of the long ears. Antlers inside the ears are invariably a disappointment if you are after a mounting deer. Antlers of either species are far more puzzling to judge when looked at from the side, and because of the forward curve in typical whitetail antlers the problem with them is compounded. The best bet for either deer if you are uncertain and are trophy hunting, is to hold out for a head on or rear on appraisal.

If you ask questions among hunter friends about deer measurements and the art of looking, you'll discover how few have put much thought or study into it, or know many answers. Nonetheless, this is a facet of deer lore often vital to success. Thorough knowledge of it makes any deer hunt more interesting, can indeed enhance your success record, and at the very least save you from some embarrassing errors.

Most common whitetail habitat is in woods edges, as here, but they have colonized diverse terrains.

This buck is in a Deep South swamp. Bottomlands of the South habor abundant whitetails.

CHAPTER 3

THE DIVERSE HABITATS
OF WHITETAILS

Whitetails of trophy size are even found in desert settings. Here hunter approaches downed buck in prickly pear cactus flat.

To a hunter, the whitetail habitat puzzle often seems impossible to decipher. It's so complicated; there's so much of it; and the deer know every bush, tree, rock, and puddle. However, the pieces can be fit together. Even though a deer may be almost anywhere in a given section of cover, most of the time it won't be. It has places where it prefers to feed, others where it rests, and habitual travel routes.

Whitetails have very definite home ranges, outside which they stray very little. A square mile does fine for most deer during their lifetimes. Sparse food or water, or the rut, may cause use of a larger range, but a couple of square miles is about the limit, and many deer live within only a quarter of that.

They follow very definite routines. Most daylight foraging and travel occurs from dawn to about 9 A.M. and again from late afternoon until dark. The deer utilize the same places day after day for movement and for resting. Weather conditions and disturbance by hunters may change their timing, and perhaps even cause them to shun their favorite sites, or change their travel routes. But the cover *types* still remain the same.

The key to cracking the whitetail cover code is to forget about the vast expanse of it and concentrate on a small section at a time, no more than a single square mile. Within that square mile several deer live permanently, and its fringes are home for several others. Much of this is used very little, but within it are those specific types of cover where the animals move and where they rest.

It might seem that this approach would fit only a place with which a whitetail hunter is familiar, since there is no such thing as "typical" whitetail habitat. The deer has done a masterful job over the centuries of colonizing amazingly diverse terrains. It lives in New England forests, southern swamps and pine savannahs, southwestern deserts, Western mountain forests, and sweeps of brushy plains. Nevertheless, the areas where whitetails feed, travel, and rest have common attributes in all their ranges around this country.

Knowing how to translate these basics from one kind of habitat to another is perhaps the most important of all whitetail hunting lore. It allows you to deduce where most of the deer will be during their active periods and during their resting periods. The entire range of the whitetail can be divided into five basic cover types. If you learn the kinds of places in each where whitetails move and rest, your success percentage anywhere you hunt will be vastly enhanced.

Farm Country with Intermittent Woods: The opening up of forests by settlement — by slicing habitat into a checkerboard of farm fields and woodlots — has formed some of the best of all whitetail range. Farm country whitetails grow big and are invariably fat. They also develop unusual wariness in order to cope with limited cover and incessant disturbance.

A good many trophy bucks live in this cover. They live long because they learn extreme wariness and because few hunters seriously ply the farm areas (some are not even aware the deer are present). The rule is that the more cover in proportion to fields, the more deer there are, and the less wary. Conversely, the less woodland, the fewer deer, but the easier it is to predict where the animals will be.

Farm country whitetail hunting is a specialist's game, and is seldom a crowded one. More of this habitat exists than is generally imagined. New York, lower New England, part of Pennsylvania, portions of all the Eastern and Southern States, southern areas of the Great Lakes States, the agricultural Midwest, and even woodlots and cornfields in the Dakotas all fit this category.

The components of farm country whitetail range are more precisely delineated than any other habitat type. The basic ones everywhere are: crop fields, empty fields, woodlots or adjoining small forests, wooded or brushy stream courses, pond or lake shores with cover, small mid-field copses, and occasional fence rows or roadsides with cover.

Empty fields can be discounted as travel routes. Their edges, where there are woods or brush borders, may offer some forage. Crop fields fall into two categories. Those with low crops, such as alfalfa, soy beans, etc., serve for night feeding grounds, and the edges that border woodlands are prime dawn and dusk feeding areas. Tall crops — corn for example — offer both forage and travel routes. The vegetation must be high enough to hide a deer so it doesn't feel uneasy moving in daylight. Once the crop is removed, of course, such a field can be discounted, except for edge feeding areas.

Only those low-growth or empty fields that have one or more sides bordered by cover will be utilized for feeding. Even then, daylight feeding will occur only in a fairly narrow swath within a few quick bounds of cover. Unbordered sides can be discounted for any daylight deer usage.

Pond and lake shores and creek or stream courses with cover are important travel routes as well as possible foraging places for deer in farm country. Not many fences or side roads offer substantial cover nowadays. However, any narrow cover strip joining two woods patches is a prime travel route. The travel possibilities, especially between unusually attractive or abundant food and woodlots or thickets, should be closely watched early and late. However, if food is plentiful along woodland borders, many farm-country deer have no need to travel precarious cover. They come out of the woods, eat, and return, showing themselves very little.

Small openings within a woodland are naturals for watching. Deer can move and feed here without ever being seen. In heavily hunted areas, a small copse out in a field may hold a wise resting buck. He goes in at dawn, stays until dusk. It's the last place a hunter would look. All the best resting places will fit that "last place" idea. They do not need to be large, just dense, and as unlikely as possible.

Gently Rolling Northern Forests: Of all whitetail cover, this is the one envisioned by most hunters as "typical." It is not mountainous. It is what many in the North and East commonly call "deer woods." It is in large forest tracts, many of them state forests or preserves in national forests. The largest expanses of these prime whitetail habitats are in New York and New England, in northern Michigan, Wisconsin, and Minnesota, northern Pennsylvania, and in the foothills of most of the Appalachian States. There is also much of it in southern Ontario, and eastward, in Canada.

This is a general mixed forest of poplar, birch, maple, oak, and beech, intermingled with various conifers: cedar, balsam, jackpine, tamarack, hemlock, and varied pines. The understory and the water-bordering stretches typically are a mixture of alder, willow, witchhazel, Juneberry, wild blackberry, and numerous other low-browse shrubs.

In these forests deer have multiple choices. There is little to restrict indiscriminate travel; watering places are never a problem, food is of infinite variety. Thus it may seem confusing to many a hunter, chiefly because it seems to have few easily definable components. A deer, presumably, can be anywhere at any time. However, the deer's-eye view is different. Only moderate portions are really useful.

This habitat type has innumerable openings. Some are large forest meadows with scattered trees. Some are miniatures, only a few yards across. In some places there may be openings formed by abandoned farms or homesteads. In most such forests, a myriad of old logging trails or more modern access trails also form long, narrow openings.

In many there are pulp-cutting or logging operations that open holes in dense forest and allow new growth to sprout. All these openings are the feeding grounds, producers of the bulk of whitetail forage. Whitetails are *edge* animals. During the early and late hours any or all these openings are the places to be watching.

The resting areas are not quite so easily defined, since the choice is broad. Nonetheless, whitetails do not feel at ease bedding or standing idly in open or sparsely vegetated places. Invariably, cover along stream courses, or around lake shores, is more dense than on the low ridges or out in the mixed forest. These, as long as they are dry or at least well drained, are important rest regions. A thicket of dense brush at the edge of an opening, or anywhere in the woods where surrounding cover is of wider-spaced trees or saplings, is a natural.

Most important of all rest areas in any weather or time of season are the strips or patches where the conifers predominate, where deciduous trees are in modest supply, or lacking entirely. Sometimes called "greenswamps" or "cedar swamps" — although not actually swampy — these offer cool, safe resting locations. Jackpine flats are included. One of these with an understory of young, low conifers in addition to mature trees is just so much the better.

Travel routes to and from these feed and rest locations are of several varieties: along the crown or base of a low ridge; following an old logging trail; around the edges of openings but always in cover; and along stream courses. A narrow swath of woods or brush between two large forest areas with openings; a place where crossing a stream is easy; a shallow saddle in a ridge — these are the top waylay places on travel routes. Don't be confused by the forest. Learn to recognize the features mentioned and forget the rest.

Forested Hill and Mountain Country: Hunters sometimes, in some places, confuse this cover with the previous one. It is true that in parts of Maine, New Hampshire, Vermont, and New York State, for example, hilly and mountainous range merges with gently rolling to flat forest country. However, deer habits in the truly steep regions differ substantially because of the addition of the prominent vertical dimension. Therefore, where the two terrain types are encountered in the same region, the hunter will immeasurably simplify his problems by separating the two in his mind, and in his hunting approach.

In addition to portions of the Northeastern U.S., this cover type is prominent all the way down the Appalachians, with hunters in the

Virginias, Tennessee, and Kentucky, North Carolina, and northern Georgia encountering it. The Texas "Hill Country," with more whitetails than any other area of the U.S., also fits this category, as do the Ozarks in Missouri and Arkansas. South Dakota's Black Hills are typical, and the same is true of northeastern Wyoming, which is an excellent whitetail range. There's more in western Montana, northern Idaho, as well as in eastern Washington.

It is true that a deer may be almost anywhere here. But most of them won't be. It is also true that weather conditions influence deer activities here more than elsewhere. Some days they'll be high up, some days a few hundred feet lower down. The general rule is that the warmer and quieter the air, the higher the deer will be, and vice versa.

If a hunter thinks in terms of imagining this terrain as flattened out, he'll understand how simple it really is. Travel routes are perhaps better defined here than anywhere else. The draws that are fairly wide at the bottom of a slope and narrow at the top should be marked down as extremely important. Invariably the cover in them is adequate. Deer move on average days from lower-elevation feeding areas uphill in the morning, and down again late in the afternoon.

Whitetails — bucks particularly — love to bed down at the uphill head of a draw. These spots are secluded, difficult to approach without detection, and escape routes go in each direction. Thus the draws, and valley openings below them, serve three hunter approaches: watching feed locations below; waylaying deer moving up or down; and still-hunting the bedding grounds.

Dense thickets midway up a slope in some mountain regions also serve for resting areas — the shady exposures when it's warm; the sunny ones on bitter mornings. But thickets atop a ridge or mesa to which one draw or more leads are the resting grounds for the majority except in high, chill winds. Overall, whitetails rest more days upslope or on top than in valleys. A notable exception: in mountains that are semi-bald or open on the slopes and tops, they bed in the brushy canyons and draw bottoms.

Feeding areas are identical to those found in rolling forest terrain — the edges and openings of small mountain-slope meadows or atop ridges or mesas, and open timber or stream edges in the valleys. In numerous locations forage is less varied than in flatter terrain, and thus the feeding grounds of consequence are easier to find. In hill and mountain cover, seek first the travel routes, including deep saddles between steep, high ridges, and they'll aim you easily to both feed and rest location.

Hardwood Bottomlands and Swamps: Except to the old-hand natives who use packs of dogs, this cover is undoubtedly the most perplexing of all whitetail ranges. Many avid deer-dog men claim, in fact, that it's impossible to hunt here without using dogs, at least in the thickest of the swamps. That's not quite true. Although a lot of bottomland and swamp cover is not readily huntable by a lone man with a gun, this actually simplifies the problem, if one keeps an open mind. Forget the vast sweeps that are too thick. Concentrate on the features that aren't. That's where most of the deer are going to be anyway!

Most of this type of cover is found across the Deep South. It properly includes Southern pine areas, usually dotted with small swamps and lakes. It begins in eastern Texas and sweeps across to the Georgia coast and through Florida. It also reaches into areas of the Mid-South, and even to eastern Arkansas and southern Illinois.

No matter how tangled the bottomland, the whitetail still remains an *edge* animal in its feeding habits. It will never be more than a mile from edges. The trick is to spot these in the confusion of the tangle. If you carefully survey a bottomland area, you quickly discover innumerable small openings. A series of these, some only a few yards across, may lie along a meander of water, or pock hardwood stands. Old trails or roads, abandoned small fields, pond shores, dry-swamp openings with grass and shrubs — these are feeding locations. Don't pass up wet places, even where water stands. Whitetails don't mind wading. Water with coarse grass growing in it often inhibits growth of large trees. The open grass, and the shrubbery along the perimeter of the openings offers forage, perfect stand spots for a hunter, and open shooting.

Resting places are invariably dense, shaded, and cool, but one rule eliminates a lot of worthless territory: a rest area must be dry. Deer dislike lying down or standing idly in water or even on soggy, seepy ground if it can be avoided. All lowlands have low ridges only a few feet high, and most swamps have higher-elevation islands or hammocks. Cover on these is usually heavy understory. These are the resting spots. A deer will wade to its belly through drowned timber out across a shallow pond to get to a high island in the center for bedding.

Travel routes show plainly — broken grass where deer wade to and from a hammock; tracked-up mud along a pond leading to a ridge. The animals avoid the impenetrable tangle just as a hunter does. The character of bottomland soil and vegetation readily imprints travel route clues. It's always more productive in this cover to hunt during the activity hours along the feeding spots and travel routes. Jumping deer from resting areas seldom offers opportunity for accurate shots.

Open & Brushy Lands: Some of the most interesting U.S. whitetail hunting is available in this cover. It's invariably confusing to hunters not native to it, for it isn't "deer woods." Yet once you evaluate it you discover that while killing a deer may be difficult, knowing where to locate them is easy. This cover type occurs in classic example in the so-called Brush Country of southern Texas, an area from which a number of trophy whitetails, and many near-trophies, have been taken. That vast sweep is flat to rolling low thornbrush and cactus, seemingly without recognizable components.

Comparable open range but differing in vegetation and general character is found in western Oklahoma, on up north through the Central Plains in portions of Kansas, Nebraska, the Dakotas, and into eastern fringes of the first tier of the Rocky Mountain States. All the open and brushy whitetail country has one important factor in common: It is relatively arid. There is ample water, but its locations are restricted, not scattered everywhere. Further, excepting the almost solid thornbrush of southern Texas, open-country whitetail range is too open for daylight activities and for bedding or resting, excepting along stream courses or ponds and lakes. That's where the cover always grows, and often is left uncut.

Over much of this habitat, even hundreds of ponds can be eliminated because there is no cover around them. Because whitetails are creatures to which cover is mandatory, the stream courses and other water surrounded by brush or trees herd them almost as if within fences. The deer may roam open fields at night, but morning and late afternoon they're never far from the brushy creeks or wooded pond sites.

Travel routes, again because whitetails won't travel in the open, are also along the stream courses. A deer in this situation hides by day in the cover along a creek, moves along it to get to a favored feeding area, and then feeds within a few bounds of the protective cover. Thus, one can discount all the vast expanse of range except where there might be water and woods or brush nearby.

Southern Texas and other areas with sweeps of unbroken brush are modestly different, but still simple, even though the kill is a real challenge. Here ranch tanks (stock ponds) or small creeks are the chief water source and magnet. Running out from every tank is what natives call a "creek," but many of these flow or are wet only during infrequent rains. However, vegetation along these low washes is always the most dense of the entire region because the most moisture is there. These so-called "creek bottoms" are the prime bedding and resting places for brush dwelling deer. They can roam anywhere to feed on the varied brush, but they cannot avoid moving to the tanks and to the dense creek-bottom cover.

In any solid-brush area, as whitetails roam to forage, they also cross any trails, ranch roads, or small openings that are present. These are prime sitting locations for hunters during the activity hours. By and large, however, when hunting open and brushy land, concentrate on the water with cover around or along it for both early and late stand hunting and midday jump shooting.

Buck during feeding time, below live oak. Acorns are among the most important foods for deer.

Piñon nuts dropped from cones like these fatten deer, but are a regionally restricted food item.

CHAPTER 4
THE DEER FORAGE FACTOR

Acorns are of wide variety, large, small, sweet, bitter. Deer eat them all, but favor certain kinds.

Despite the countless reams of deer-hunting lore available, the most vital single factor related to hunting success is seldom emphasized enough. It concerns what a deer eats. The most important activity of a deer's day is filling its stomach, and probably 90 percent of deer bagged every season anywhere on the continent are tagged on their way to a feeding area, while feeding, or while moving from feeding to resting places.

A deer biologist friend, researching favored foods of whitetails in the county where I live, impressed upon me a decade ago the relationship of deer diet to hunting success. It changed the emphasis of my own hunting procedures.

"Depending on the size of the individual deer," he told me, "from 10 to as much as 20 pounds of forage are required to fill its paunch. It has to make this effort at least twice every twenty-four hours. That's a lot of browse, acorns, weeds. While gathering a paunchful, deer must move around. Forgetting special activities such as the rut, it is during their feeding activities that deer are most exposed and vulnerable to hunters."

Every deer doesn't necessarily stuff itself every time it eats. Routinely in normal seasons deer feed heavily from predawn until an hour or two after. They then find a comfortable resting place, lie down, and chew their cud. They get up intermittently, feed a bit, change bed locations for better shade, perhaps, then in mid to late afternoon begin to feed seriously again.

Deer may drink after feeding in the morning, or in warm weather in the middle of the day. Water, however, is seldom a problem, nor is a special trek to water usually necessary. I've watched both mule deer and whitetails on numerous occasions pause for a drink on their way to bed after morning feeding, and pause again for a drink on the way from resting cover to heavy afternoon foraging.

The problem that most deer hunters have regarding deer foods is that most published information on the subject is in the form of long lists. They're meaningless and confusing to an individual hunter unless he sorts out what applies to the area he hunts. Both whitetails and mule deer eat scores of different kinds of vegetation and their products. Deer could not have colonized so widely without being tolerant of a highly varied diet. But among many forage items, only a few are abundant enough in any given area to tie deer down to them for repeated feedings over a period of time.

Regional favorites among deer foods often wrongly influence hunters over wide range. An old hand at mule deer hunting in New Mexico once explained to me that stands of piñon drew mule deer more certainly than any other food. He was correct, with qualifications. I've killed several mule deer that were feeding under nut-loaded piñons. The catch is, they grow only in specific portions of the southern Rockies, the Southwest, and Mexico. Elsewhere there are none. The old apple orchard in New England is a similar example. It may be a great place — there — but in a Louisiana swamp or the Arizona desert, there are abundant deer but no apples. In other words, what is important is the deer diet *where you hunt.*

Further, prominent favorite deer forage may change in only a few miles. Where I live there are many oaks of several varieties. Deer browse them and eat the acorns. A hundred miles south there are no oaks, only thornbrush and cactus. Specific areas there have abundant *huajillo,* a feathery-leaved shrub that is prime deer forage. In my region we have none.

Prominent diet items can differ over much shorter distances. Mark this well. I remember hunting with an old gentleman in northern Michigan who almost without fail filled his tag in his own farm woodlot, which was a solid stand of maple with heavy sapling growth among the larger trees. He claimed, correctly, that deer are avid for maple browse; that's why he was successful. Less than 3 miles away was a large expanse of state forest, most of it mixed poplar, white birch, and conifers. I hunted there, and my successes were based entirely on poplar.

One should not be misled either by summer or early-fall preseason scouting trips, which many hunters insist are paramount to success. In summer deer eat large amounts of green, succulent foods (even the form of their droppings in summer indicate this diet). But as summer wanes and fall proceeds toward winter, green food in most latitudes is either frosted or seasonally dies down. What had been green, moist foods become brown and dry. Lush green grass may have appealed to deer for a portion of their diet, but dry grass is eaten only under the poorest of range conditions, a starvation diet.

There is a most important bit of seasonal diet lore in this. After frosts and the fall die-down of forbs, grasses, and vines, deer diet must change drastically. But they will always seize the opportunity to take any green food that remains available. In my area, for example, every small ranch has patches of winter oats, rye grass, or Bermuda that remain green all deer season. Deer swarm out of cover along the edges of these fields daily to eat the green shoots. Wherever there are succulents available for deer after the normal "green" season, they are magnets.

One caution relative to preseason scouting concerns seasonal favorites such as regionally abundant wild fruits. In early fall I've seen chokecherry and wild black cherry trees with low limbs paved at their base with deer droppings, the fruit stripped from every reachable branch. This concentrated sign can excite a hunter. However, fall fruits will be long gone when most deer seasons open.

Late fall, one must realize, is a time of drastic change for the deer, an adjustment period in their manner of making a living, a radical change of diet. A few years ago, pondering the importance of the food equation, I made a numbered list to help guide me. No. 1 and No. 2 we've already examined: what deer foods are present where you hunt, and which are available when you hunt? No. 3 begins to whittle deer diet down to fine focus, and may spell the difference between success and none: What deer foods are available *this season* in your specific hunting area?

A New York friend hunted a large thornapple thicket every fall for four years. He collected a buck every season and had the place staked out as his "deer corral." The fifth year the trees failed to bear. The deer knew this long before season opened, but the hunter had failed to check. There wasn't a sign of a deer, and he was at a loss at the last minute where to hunt.

This same oversight occurs in scores of places annually because hunters are so fond of repeating that deer love acorns and beechnuts, so oak and beech trees is where you'll find deer. But oaks and beeches don't produce a nut crop every year. In my area I've seen the ground literally paved under a live oak or a black jack with acorns, and watched deer stand in one spot and fill up in 20 minutes. The following year the same trees bore not an acorn and deer paid no attention to them.

Certain oaks — shin oak, for example — grow as low brush, and deer can browse twigs and leaves (in some areas a favored forage), and eat acorns during seasons the oaks bear right off the tree. Those low-growing oaks therefore are good bets for watching whether or not acorns are present. Conversely, large oaks are seldom important browse because deer can't reach the twigs and leaves. And even though there may be a good acorn crop, it's possible *your* deer season may fall before the acorns do, and the deer will pass up the oaks because they can't get the acorns until they drop to ground. In other words, the hunter who focuses his hunting techniques on deer diet should know as much about oaks and acorns — and other deer favorites — as about deer.

This gets us to No. 4 on my list of guidelines: which of the several food items in your hunting area do the deer *like* best? A bit more about acorns serves to illustrate how you can zero in. Even though all acorns are prime deer food, the animals like some kinds better than others. There are two large groups of oaks: white and red. The acorns of red oaks are bitter; those of white oaks, sweet. Deer eat both, but prefer the latter. When acorns are generally abundant, white oaks get the bigger play.

Deer even show preferences for the larger acorns when choices are available. You can enhance your success by watching specific trees. On our ranch we have five kinds of oaks. The largest, sweetest acorns are from chestnut oaks, trees that don't bear every year. They also are invariably in minority numbers. This makes it easy to mark down locations of individual trees, as there are no groves, or stands. During heavy crop seasons, deer make beelines for these trees in preference to other oaks, once the acorns are down. They can fill up faster and with less effort on these tastiest of acorns beneath our few chestnut oaks. Over the years we've put several deer in the freezer because we learned about this preference.

That favorite-food-availability guideline obviously applies to numerous items of deer diet. Other examples are the out-of-season succulents previously mentioned, waste grains in farm country, and forest cuttings where new aspen, birch, maple, and other browse trees have sprouted. Guideline No. 5 is simply a refinement of No. 4: which of the foods favored when you're hunting is present *in most ample supply*?

If you're a bowhunter in the early season, it could be those chokecherry bushes or wild black cherry trees. If you're a late-season mule deer hunter in territory where muleys migrate from high country to lower-altitude winter range, it might be sage, bitterbrush, manzanita. These would be classed as "favorites" related to that time and place. Perhaps they're the only abundant forage present. In deep northern snows whitetails may be forced to select as "favorite" forage jackpine or cedar, and to bunch up in stands of those trees. If you're hunting then, these equate with most-ample-supply.

Guideline No. 6 concerns tying deer down for the longest periods per day, hopefully throughout the season, to certain predictable places. Which foods are available abundantly in *specific areas*, so that deer head straight to them and do most of their foraging within a modest expanse, rather than wandering and picking tidbits here and there? Those green winter oat fields surrounded by woods, clear-cut forests, or Western ridges heavy with mountain mahogany (a favorite muley food), or dense patches of shin oak brush — all are good examples.

There is a final consideration for the hunter who uses knowledge of deer diet to help him score. During seasons following a severe summer drought, deer food is scarce. This may not produce extra-fat deer, but it does bring higher success to those who watch feeding areas. The animals have to work harder and longer to make their living. They thus are vulnerable for longer periods. And they may become tied to certain forage because it's all they have, which makes finding them easier.

On the other hand, in some instances they may simply have to wander farther, grabbing whatever they can find. This won't bring them to exact locations for long, but it will force them more into the open, leading them to or across predictable general areas where they eventually can fill up.

The hunter who'll follow the guidelines proposed here, and make a thorough study of deer foods on hand in the area where and when he hunts, will almost certainly up his score. Once you realize that the entire life of a deer revolves around its stomach, your chances of filling your freezer will improve.

Fall mushrooms are relished by deer. These boletes are one of the favorites.

We discovered that days when TV receptions was excellent deer wandered intermittently in our yard all day.

CHAPTER 5

LIVING WITH WHITETAILS

Bucks select certain saplings and bushes for making rubs. These differ area to area.

On a bright fall afternoon the day before deer season opened several years ago, I sat in my office, working and intermittently looked out the windows, observing two whitetail deer that were combing the areas under oak trees in our yard. Curious about what they were after, I picked up a pair of binoculars.

Under the oaks I discovered clusters of large, fat, brown bolete mushrooms had pushed up. Boletes are of several species, most of them edible and delicious to humans as well as deer. In numerous areas they are among the most abundant fall mushrooms. The deer, out foraging in broad daylight, seemed to know the boletes would not last long. Some would quickly decay, and insects would riddle others. Various mushrooms, I knew, were relished by deer; as one hunter friend puts it, they serve as a kind of seasonal dessert.

As I watched, I was envisioning horse trails along woods edges on our ranch, a remote piece of land 20 miles from our home place, where my office is. Deer regularly follow the trails made by horses. During falls when boletes are abundant, these mushrooms invariably spring up in patches and rows along the travel routes. If boletes were appearing right now in our yard, they were undoubtedly popping up along those trails on the ranch.

The next morning at dawn I was out there on a stand where I could scan one of the trails, having verified the previous evening that indeed the bolete crop was showing abundantly here. Signs indicated that some early ones had been eaten. Ample numbers were left, and probably more would appear before morning. At exactly 8:00 A.M., a fat forkhorn came tripping along the trail, picking off boletes as he traveled. Shortly after, he was hanging from the meat pole in our old creekside camp.

Obviously this is not an experience one is likely to repeat year after year. But what it demonstrates is that close and constant observation of deer may turn up deer habits that can be applied to hunting. For more than twenty-five years I have practically lived with whitetails. Hardly a day passes when I'm home that I don't have the opportunity to watch and wonder about what the deer are doing. Our home place consists of 27 heavily wooded acres, with two ponds. For years, subdivisions from our nearby growing city have been crowding in on the area. Our land has become a kind of oasis for resident deer. Year after year we have from six to a dozen. They wander off this reservation at night, but most of their lives are spent in our small woods because all around us the cover has been stripped.

Although we give these deer supplemental feed in winter and during droughty summers, they're not tame. We purposely avoid trying to make them so. Thus I can observe wild whitetails on a small range, day after day. One lesson I've learned from this constant contact is to be wary of pronouncements on the nature of whitetails, whether from biologists who do studies or oldtimey hunters who claim to know all about deer.

Much *has* been learned by specific research, but deer are infinitely complicated creatures, and the "final secrets" of whitetail behavior and hunting success are still being learned. Just when you begin to think you have whitetail lore down pat, some behavior will astonish you, and try as you might, you won't be able to explain the why of it.

For instance, in the hilly country where we live, we get abominable TV reception most of the time, and have no opportunity for cable hookup. One noon I switched on the TV to watch the news, and here was a sharp, clear, stable picture. We were into one of our "good TV" periods, which usually last two or three days.

I happened to look out the window while the news was on, and saw deer wandering all over the yard. Suddenly I wondered: was there some correlation? The following noon, a Friday, I switched on the TV, found the picture still sharp. Again the deer were moving around. That evening both my sons got home for a hunt down on the ranch the next day. I told them about the TV and the noon activity of the deer. When they came back from the ranch on Sunday evening, they related that deer had moved most of the day, both days. They each had easily filled tags. Monday noon I checked the TV. Bad. I also checked the deer. Not one showed.

I don't pretend to know what relationship there is between excellent noncable TV reception and deer movement. The TV service people blame both good and bad reception on "atmospheric conditions," whatever that means. I do know that further checks over several seasons showed that the phenomenon occurred quite consistently. We always try nowadays to get a chance to hunt on good TV days, and are seldom disappointed with deer movement.

One of the problems with patterning your hunting on research is that it may not be universally applicable. This is not to put down research, but only to caution you about accepting any too-pat theories as your bible.

I recall some years ago a study done in the East "proving" that whitetail deer do not eat grass. Following it, one writer rehashed the report and warned hunters to shy from grassy situations and hunt only where browse was available. In my area, where deer and Bermuda grass are both abundant, it is not unusual to see several dozen deer gorging themselves in fall on lush and succulent Bermuda. Where the study was done, the statement that deer don't eat grass might have been valid, but not where I live. "Always" and "everywhere" take in a *lot* of territory. What's important is to know the habits of deer in *your* area.

As an example, on numerous occasions in fall when the rut is starting, I've had opportunity to watch a buck making a scrape. Recently, near dusk, I saw a six-pointer within 60 steps of the kitchen windows. A wide-spreading live oak there has some branches that droop to within less than 4 feet of the ground. The buck reached up to nuzzle twigs and leaves on a branch and gently stroke them with his antler tips, then began to paw out a scrape.

Later he fiddled with a large cedar, nuzzling and stroking it with his antlers, but he did not paw the ground. I have checked scrapes many times in our area, and seldom are they made anywhere except under live oaks, where a branch droops within nuzzling reach. Never have I found one under a Texas cedar. Both trees are tremendously abundant in my area. When I set out to look for scrapes, I check the live oaks. It's a shortcut, quite often, to a successful hunt.

Whitetails are also selective, my home-place observations have taught me, about what tree or shrub species they use for rubs. We watch for rubs here at home to keep a check on where the bucks are hanging out, hoping they don't move off the reservation and get shot. With few exceptions they select small cedars — actually Ashe junipers. On the ranch, that's where we search for rubs of bucks we hope to get a chance to shoot.

But I carried rub observations farther. I remembered that in northern Michigan, where I once lived, most deer used small balsams for rubbing. However, I once found an area there where witch hazel bushes were abundant, and for some reason bucks used those, in that location, more than they used conifers. Out of curiosity about whether Texas deer would do something similar, I scoured our home place, seeking rubs on other than cedars. One hillside has an abundance of Texas persimmon, a tough, smooth-barked shrub. I discovered that our home bucks often made rubs on these. I thereafter scanned persimmon patches on the ranch because there were not many of these, but thousands of cedars. I caught a buck in the act and whacked him. Once more what I'd learned by living with deer had paid off.

Not many hunters will have a situation comparable to mine for deer watching. Most can, however, find public lands, even wildlife refuges (which are often excellent locations), where they can make a hobby of observing deer off and on all year. Fall and winter are the best times, because deer habits change with the seasons. Months that coincide with or bracket open season will be prime times for learning much that will apply to hunting success.

Always be alert for unique activities. You can bone up on basics by reading books and magazines. A classic example of what I have in mind concerns two gems learned from deer in our yard. Whenever there is unusual deer activity during daylight hours, I always try to ferret out what may have caused it. Several years ago during a time when the deer seemed especially active much of the day for several days in a row, I was browsing through an almanac and suddenly realized that these activity days had fallen during and immediately after the equinox.

This got me fired up and wondering also about what might happen during the winter solstice. Sure enough, the same kind of activity occurred. We've checked these periods on the ranch for several years, and so far, deer movement has matched that of the home deer.

The amount of *movement* of deer is directly related to hunter success. The more they move, the more they are visible, and the higher hunters score. The greatest amount of movement is during feeding periods. It has been said many times that whitetails eat such a variety of foods that seldom does any one variety tie them to a specific place. Meticulous observation of feeding deer disproves that.

I've watched deer feeding in a small open valley near our house for long periods. It is grassy, and my first assumption was that they were indiscriminately eating grass of several varieties. However, I was skeptical.

I studied what was going on through binoculars. The deer would take a bite, move a step or two and take another. I was able to see wads of grass in their mouths. There is a tough, abrasive grass in my area locally called "wire grass." That, and only that, is what the deer were eating. Applying that to hunting, we've staked out (twice now successfully) grassy areas on our ranch where bunches of wire grass are scattered. On every whitetail range, I'm sure, a keen-eyed hunter can discover certain obscure forage that deer relish. This advanced lore reaches far past the basics of acorns and hardwood browse, and if diligently pursued, sometimes can make the difference between success and failure.

Classic examples occur where certain foods occur erratically; a heavy crop one season and none at all for the next several years. In my area wild grapes make a good crop only now and then. We have lots of wild grapevines at home and my wife likes to make jelly when they bear. We have to check closely in order to beat the deer to them.

Another most interesting phenomenon I've observed is that there are distinct individual tastes and food habits among deer. The cedar, or juniper, that covers the Texas Hill Country where I live bears masses of bluish berries in some years. I've watched our home deer around them many times. Certain individuals that we easily recognize seem simply addicted to them. Others totally spurn them. I've killed deer and opened paunches that are packed with these berries, while others in the same season have none.

Looking back over the many years of living with these deer and their progeny, I realize that they've taught us countless lessons. When relative humidity is low, the deer move more than when it is high. On days when the temperature is normal for that time of year, or lower, movement is greater than when it is higher. A hard, chill rain dampens our deer movement, but a mist or drizzle, especially at normal temperature, sees them moving about, and not as wary as on bright days. When winds blow, we don't see deer.

Indeed, according to my observations, weather undoubtedly has the greatest influence on deer movement. I sometimes wonder if these home-place deer, which have it pretty good, are aware of all they've taught me about how to bag their ranch brethren. If so, maybe one day they'll begin passing me false leads!

When a buck looks fully alert and raises one front foot, that's a signal it probably is about to run.

There's no question about what a fully raised flag means.

CHAPTER 6
WHITETAIL BODY LANGUAGE

When a feeding deer raises its head and stares at you, stand immobile. Watch its tail. A quick flick side to side is the ''all clear'' signal. It will resume feeding.

It was not the size of the whitetail buck that intrigued me and kept my glass glued to it, but its actions. It was a modest-sized, eight-point at about 150 yards. When I first saw it walking broadside, there was something in its manner of movement that seemed to indicate it knew precisely where it was going.

A few steps farther, it paused and put its head down briefly as if smelling the ground. Then it arched its neck and moved its head back and forth, not in an agitated manner but almost gently. I could see that the tips of one antler touched a small, leafy branch directly overhead. It was not trying to rip at or fight the branch, as antler-polishing bucks do. Next in the sequence, it reached its muzzle upward and nuzzled the same small branch, not feeding but simply brushing the twig with its nose.

After the buck finally left the spot, my curiosity led me over there. What I found was a scrape, unquestionably the most important buck sign a hunter can discover. That experience occurred over 20 years ago. It was the first time I had ever located a buck scrape in that fashion. Over the years, however, I have spotted big bucks repeating this performance. By recognizing the antic, I was able later to take a stand near the scrape and conclude my hunt.

You might term such observations the study of the body language of whitetails. They exhibit many movements, stances and physical signs that relay to an astute hunter their intent. A study of this language is a kind of advanced course in whitetail hunting. Knowing the various nuances of movement meanings and using them to one's own advantage can easily double success percentage.

You cannot, however, be a sloppy observer. It requires watching deer, by the hour, at varied seasons and under differing conditions of weather to catalog all the useful knowledge of their bodily movements and to be certain of proper interpretations. This applies to does just as much as to bucks. In many states there are antlerless quotas. Regardless, it is all too often the doe you have to watch in order to get past her defenses to a shot at the buck.

One of the most valuable experiences for a hunter is to get into the woods without a gun, find a few stands where deer can be watched and stay with them. Even making trial stalks, movements or sounds to purposely alert them allows you to see their reactions and to become adept at predicting what they intend to do next.

When I came to Texas to live some years ago, my first deer hunting was done on a ranch in the hill country where blinds on stilts with numerous comforts are common. Frankly, sitting in a blind and not being able to move when I wished bored me stiff. But after a little of it, I began to realize that this was a great opportunity to study deer.

It was from such a blind that I watched a very presentable buck actually making and thereafter visiting a scrape. I held fire because I wanted to learn. Because some readers may not know much about this all-important sign, I'll briefly describe the movements of the deer. It selected a spot at the edge of cover on reasonably soft ground and with that inevitable branch at antler height overhead. It raked the earth with front hoofs over an area below its belly and to a depth of a couple inches.

Now it urinated in the soft earth and on its own hocks, scraped the resultant mud around, nosed the ground, plucked at the over-hanging twig and finally moved on. This sign, made during the rut, is a domain marker. A buck may make several around his home bailiwick. They tell interloper bucks to beware and tell area does that the old gent is at home and in a breeding mood.

I watched the buck come back to that scrape three days in a row. Meanwhile, I watched several different does visit it. Nose down, each examined the spot. A couple simply moved on. This signified that they were not ready to be bred. But several others paused to urinate in the same spot, leaving a calling card for the next round of the buck, then went away, obviously hoping to be pursued. The actions of the does, even if I had not seen the buck make the scrape, would have told me — once I'd learned about them — that it was there. Any hunter who is out during the rut, observes a doe at such actions, or the buck as I have described, has a tailor-made collection point for the winter's venison.

The ears of whitetail deer are extremely expressive. The senses of smell and hearing are acute, and while deer spot movement instantly, they have difficulty correctly appraising immobile objects. Thus, when any sense is alerted, all are zeroed in. A deer that sees something suspicious in its surroundings cocks its ears forward to listen intently. When the ears are at full cock, and the deer is looking toward you, it is obvious you'd better freeze and make no sound.

If one ear switches backward, then the deer turns its head to cock its ear and zero its vision toward other points, you know it is uncer-tain. Stay silent and immobile, but bet there's a 50–50 chance that the animal is not really suspicious of you. It simply is uneasy because something is wrong. When the ears relax and the deer looks away or puts its head down, you are probably safe to carefully continue a stalk.

If you see a feeding doe lay its ears flat back and rear up, you know she has companions, other does, probably fawns and possibly a spike or forkhorn buck. Groups of whitetails seldom contain a mature buck in the fall, and there is invariably one crotchety old doe in the bunch who rears and strikes at others with her front hoofs. If you'll settle for a small buck, spotting a doe acting so may mean one is somewhere around in the group, still tagging its mother. If you don't see one soon, however, leave. A bossy old doe is also the worst tattle-tale in the whitetail crowd.

One of my favorite hunting methods during the rut is rattling up bucks with a pair of antlers prepared for the purpose to simulate a buck fight. One of the lessons in body language I learned early is never to give up or be disgusted if a giddy little spike comes running up to your hideout. Watch its ears intently. Nothing so infuriates a mature buck as to have some pipsqueak interloper in its domain during breeding season. Bucks may assume that the simulated fight is over a doe.

A spike will run in without caution, back off, prance around, timid yet longing. A couple of years ago, I had one on hand acting this way. Suddenly I saw it cock one ear backward, turn its head and look behind and to its right, ears at full cock. Those ear motions were a dead giveaway. I got my rifle ready and looked where the spike was looking. The spike's ears went back and it whirled and ran off. It had no intention of tangling with Mr. Big. An arrogant looking ten-pointer immediately trotted in.

Then there is the ear action of a doe during breeding season. You are on a stand, let's say, and you see a doe move out of the brush to cross a small open area. She isn't running. Instead, she seems to glide out. Then she stops, looks around, and cocks one ear back, listening behind her. You know nothing has frightened her. She moves a few steps and back goes that ear again. Watch the spot in the brush out of which she came. There's a buck following her. If she moves on across and into cover, he may emerge head to the ground, nose on her track, so don't be looking only at antler height. If she waits in the open, he will probably emerge with head up.

By some uncanny sense, whitetails are able to recognize the sounds of others of their kind walking over rocks or making other noisy movements, and they also quickly spot other deer, even distantly moving through thickets. A feeding or lazing whitetail has a very distinctive stance when it looks at another deer. The ears are up and cocked, but they are bent far forward, and there is no tense or rigid contraction of leg and body muscles.

Often I have watched a doe fiddling along and suddenly seen her turn her head and stare intently off at an angle, but without any evidence whatever of concern. A sharp hunter will learn to recognize this stance and curiosity instantly. The deer is plainly saying that another deer is over there. Often, of course, the attention has been drawn by scent coming down or across wind toward both the deer under observation and the hunter. The other deer may be another doe. It may also be the big buck you want. This recognition of their own kind is not the same as during the rut. The deer may have no interest in breeding, nor in joining the other or others. It's simply the casual recognition of an acquaintance.

There are several varied movements of the head and front feet that tell much of a whitetail's state of mind. Many hunters may have seen how a doe, staring intently at their position, may stretch her neck and stiffly move her head from side to side several times, shifting weight from one front leg to the other. As she does this, her ears are at full cock. She is totally alert. Bucks occasionally do this.

This head sign means the deer is genuinely disturbed, but it also means it is not really sure. Deer are color-blind, thus living in a world of shades from black to white. In addition, its eyes are set so that it sees best straight ahead. Because of the lack of color in its vision, there is somewhat less depth perception. The scene it views is flatter than what the hunter sees. The head movement is an attempt to sharpen edges of objects being studied by slightly changing the viewing angle. You have to be extra careful when you see this movement. The deer may be on the verge of flight.

The stamped forefoot is another bit of language important for a hunter to learn. A simulation of the sound has been used on occasion during rut to bring in a buck, but this is risky business. Ordinarily a deer that is uneasy first raises a foreleg and holds it momentarily with the lower leg bent slightly backward. This means, "What's going on out there?" Then the foot comes down hard. This says that anxiety is growing, but it also may be an attempt by the animal to make the danger, whatever it is, give itself away.

Watch closely, and you may quite often note that a deer that stamps its foot several times will then walk very slowly and stiffly toward your position, at least a few steps. If it is a doe, which is likely, and there is a buck anywhere around, you're in bad shape. This deer is determined to find out what you are and probably will.

On occasion you may see a buck running with its mouth open. I recall with amusement hunting with a friend who had seen this and told me something obviously had been chasing the deer. It was so tired it didn't even hold its tail up, he said, and was gasping for breath. It was undoubtedly tired all right, but it wasn't being chased. It was chasing. A rutting buck often chases a doe with its mouth open and slobbering. Instead of giving up on such a deer that zips out of sight, get yourself right into the area and wait. Pursued does commonly circle. There's an excellent chance she may bring her avid pursuer right back around to your crosshair.

Of all whitetail body language, unquestionably the various movements of the tail are the most important to properly interpret. This is the flag that is raised and waved from side to side in flight, possibly to alert others to do likewise. At least, you can bet that deer on one hillside that see waving flags on the opposite slope will also flee. From the use of the tail so emphatically to indicate the presence of danger (an ever present need) a whole series of tail expressions has evolved.

The whitetail is an exceedingly nervous creature. The deer puts its head down, takes a bite, jerks the head up, flicks the ears this way and that. It stares and perhaps whirls around. When a bird flutters or a grasshopper flies up, the deer flushes in panic only to pause and come back almost foolishly. Seldom does a whitetail forage more than a few seconds without raising its head to look around.

When you are making a stalk, or watching deer and hoping for a shot, don't concentrate completely on the head. Watch the tail. Let's say the deer jerks up its head and stares right at you. Perhaps it continues to stare, utterly motionless, for several minutes. You think you can't hold your position another second. Suddenly the tail makes a single switch — flick, flick. Immediately or very shortly afterward the deer will lower its head again.

That little switch is an all-clear sign. Let out your breath and continue your stalk until the head raises again. The flick of the tail seems to be almost like a turning off of attention. It is close to infallible as a sign in your favor. However, if a deer continues to stare and stretch its neck, then switches its tail nervously, and several times with a second or two in between, the message is exactly opposite. This is an animal beginning to be quite uneasy.

Sometimes it happens that a hunter is desperately trying to get in position for a shot. Tail action, if closely observed, can indicate how much time he'll have. When a deer raises the tail to about straight out behind while staring or moving nervously, time is short. The animal has its mind made up that things are getting serious. When the tail moves a little above horizontal and over to one side, don't bet on more than a second or two longer. From that slant, it is thrown straight up, the animal wheels, probably snorting and plunges away with flag waving.

The only time the news is good from a tail held straight out behind is when a buck is at the peak of the rut. On a number of hunts, I've seen a buck running fast, out of range, running, not bounding, and a quick glassing showed the tail stiffly straight out behind. Just as when seeing a buck running with its mouth open, get into the area as fast as possible. There's a chance a widely circling doe may bring the chase back around and put the eager buck into easy range.

Earlier, I mentioned not only movements as body language, but also stance. The way a deer stands indicates on scores of occasions when you cannot see antlers, whether it is a buck or a doe. Sometimes brush background confuses the sight picture, or the animal is simply too far away. Think of the body of a buck standing broadside as presenting a somewhat rectangular shape. A broadside doe looks more like a low-tilted triangle, the neck and withers forming the apex.

A whitetail doe, facing you, appears very thin across the chest; the forelegs seem to splay outward, again forming a triangle, upright with the apex at the throat. The forelegs of a buck come down straighter to the ground. His chest is broader. If you practice looking long and carefully through a glass at deer, you become adept at telling with fair accuracy at a glance and at long range whether the animal is a buck or doe. This is valuable knowledge. A deer moving into cover may give you only a glance, but you'll be able to assess whether, if you're hunting a buck, it is worth going after.

Not only will the study of whitetail body language help to fine-tune your hunting ability, but it is an immensely intriguing hobby by itself. You discover that watching to learn movement meanings is almost on an excitement par with the actual shooting. You hold fire "this one time" to see what a movement of a certain deer indicates it intends to do next, so you can use the knowledge to outwit the next one, if you don't forget to shoot because of watching that one too!

Mule deer are placid characters. This modest buck watches photographer, but without alarm.

Does bed down in dry wash under shady tree without attempting to hide. The position of their big ears signifies curiosity, but no alarm.

CHAPTER 7

THE MULE DEER PERSONALITY

Even in this fairly open area hunter was able to stalk buck within easy range.

One of the most widely experienced big-game hunters I've known told me when I was a beginner, "Every animal has its own distinctive personality. Becoming acquainted with it is the key to hunting success."

The importance of that observation was especially impressed upon me when I began hunting mule deer. By then I had a decade of whitetail experience. It suddenly dawned that deer weren't just deer. Traits and reactions of muleys, compared to the whitetails I'd known, were totally different.

One of my early experiences illustrates in an exaggerated manner my lack of knowledge of muley personality, and how it differs from that of the whitetail. I was hunting in Wyoming with a rancher. We jumped a good buck from a gully, and it bounded at top speed up the bordering ridge. Overeager, I shot and missed. The deer churned on up to the crest. There it stopped, stood broadside, looking back. The rancher cautioned me not to shoot at it skylined. No bullet backstop.

Spang in the open, it stared down at us. I couldn't believe it. No whitetail would ever do that. Presently it whirled and bounded on over, as if revving up to run clear out of the country.

Embarrassed at my foul-up, I said, "I guess we'll have to find another."

The rancher said, "Oh, there's a good chance we can get that one if you want it. It's a good buck."

We started up the open ridge. Near the crown, which had only a single bush offering any cover, he indicated I should remove my hat and crawl behind it. When I finally peeked through the branches, there was the buck, nibbling at some forage possibly 150 yards distant. To it, danger had come and gone. Out of sight, out of mind.

It would be all too easy to conclude from such an experience that mule deer are plain dumb. They certainly are more vulnerable than whitetails, as all deer managers concluded long ago. They cannot stand the hunting pressure the whitetail can, but it's doubtful this is a matter of lack of intelligence. It hinges simply on mule deer personality. The muley is a placid, stolid, deliberate animal. It is also a true wilderness creature that never has made peace with man's settlement (to which the whitetail has so strikingly adapted) and doesn't know how. It is naive, and too curious at times for its own good.

"A whitetail runs, never knowing what spooked it," one naturalist has said, "but a mule deer often can't resist looking back to identify the source of its fright."

The whitetail also keeps on running, perhaps over three ridges before it stops. But unless a mule deer is severely frightened, one ridge usually suffices. The mule deer isn't a worrier. Compared to it, the whitetail is a neurotic. Once I had the unusual opportunity in northeastern Wyoming, where both species are present, to observe a whitetail and a muley on the same slope feeding about 100 yards apart.

The muley pottered along, unconcerned. The whitetail would take a bite, throw up its head, flick its ears in every direction, start to lower its head, jerk it up again, repeating endlessly. Watching it wore *me* out. The only time the mule deer seemed disturbed was when a small bird flew out of a bush near the whitetail, which shied wildly, then stood snorting and blowing. The mule deer cocked its big ears toward the other deer, stared momentarily, apparently puzzled, then went about its business.

It occurred to me recently that in some thirty-five years of mule deer hunting, in states all the way from the Canadian to the Mexican border, I have yet to hear a mule deer blow nervously like a whitetail. I've seen scores of them stand and stare at me, but I've never witnessed one stamping a foot, as whitetails commonly do.

Don't construe such lack of concern to mean muleys can't be canny. Old bucks are masters at leading the private life. Yet they do it with simple directness, moving back, back as far as they can get from disturbance. That's where experienced trophy hunters operate. Conversely, a crafty, jittery, secretive old trophy whitetail may live right under civilization's nose in a farm woodlot and never be suspected by anyone.

A hunter friend has an interesting theory that just looking at each species and watching them run tells you much about their differing personalities. "The mule deer, broadside, looks blocky, rectangular, heavy-legged, big-footed, like a range bull," he says. "It appears practical, direct, stoic. A whitetail looks far more delicate, always tense, slender of leg, dainty of hoof, devious, ever mistrusting. When the whitetail runs all out, its hind feet reach far past where the fores come down, pushing frantically, getting it the heck away in frenzied flight. The mule deer's rear feet strike behind the fronts — awesome power but not the emphasis on haste."

Long ago I concluded that mule deer, sometimes giving the appearance of stupidity, are in fact basically erratic and unpredictable. They don't know what they're going to do until they do it. You can predict with fair certainty where a whitetail will hide, which way it will run, where it will bed. Both hiding and bedding locations will almost always be where the deer may not be able to see out, but you can't see in either.

Mule deer invariably hide or go to bed where they can see all around.
That's an important rule for finding them. But don't even try to predict
where, except very generally — which means search everywhere. Many
mule deer are overlooked by hunters who skim past all the places where
they wouldn't expect a deer, and there's a chance that's where the deer
may be.

I learned from expert natives in mule deer country over the years
never to fail to glass the single bush out on an open ridge, to peer into
deep shadow under the smallest juniper, to watch for the head or antlers
of a buck silhouetted against yellow grass as it lies under a single piñon
on an open slope. Old bucks especially love to lie on a secluded ledge
on a point overlooking a valley, and usually have two opposite-direction
escape routes if anything disturbs them.

Whitetails venture into or along edges of open areas with utmost
reluctance. When they do they utilize every bush, weed, and sapling to
sneak behind. Mule deer are unafraid of open areas. In fact, some of
the best muley hunting, often overlooked, is in virtually treeless Western
foothill regions. Especially in foothill and desert terrain they habitually
feed along nearly coverless slopes. Most hunters don't look there. If
the deer are disturbed, they don't necessarily retreat into dense cover,
or sneak cleverly around. They simply — and with practical good sense
— move back two more ridges and go on browsing again in the same
type of terrain.

Unpredictability is most evident when mule deer become aware
of the presence of the hunter. I witnessed the demise of a big buck
one fall in Utah because upon seeing two of us horsebacking along
a slope it trotted a few feet, backed under drooping pine branches,
and stood, head lowered, to peer out. On that same hunt I came on
a deer I didn't want that stared at me at short range long enough to
have been skinned and butchered. Then for no logical reason it suddenly all but turned wrong side out. It bolted, went off the ridge
into an open flat and was still running when it was a mile away. Only
the buck knew why.

Mule deer often seem to presume naively that they're hidden when
they're not. This is a personality trait, I'm convinced, not simple errors
of judgement. In Arizona I watched a desert muley run away from me
up a slope where only a few yuccas grew. All it had to do was go over
the crest and be gone. Instead, halfway, it whirled behind a slender
yucca, lay down facing back, and stretched its head out flat. I stalked
a buck in western Texas one fall, got within 100 yards, then decided

against taking it. The deer, watching closely and immobile all that time, at last sank in laughable slow motion to the ground and lay down, still partly visible behind a Spanish dagger.

A curious trait hunters should always be alert to is illustrated by an experience I've encountered several times. Driving with a friend in a 4WD, we jumped a big ten-pointer from under a trailside bush. It ran full tilt up the adjacent slope in the open. I bailed out, racked in a cartridge, and missed the deer. Another few bounds while I was regrouping would have put it over the open crest and into timber on the other slope. Instead, the deer cut behind a small patch of oak brush with leaves still on and dived from the rear back toward us, into the oak. I could hear brush crackle and see it move. There the buck stood, immobile, in easy range, head and neck deeply shadowed but still a target. Why they commit these unpredictable acts I'm convinced even the deer don't know until the notion strikes. In general mule deer prefer to hide, or pretend to, rather than run far, whereas whitetails will run far and then hide.

Hunters who depend on the volatile, glassy-eyed, frenzied actions of whitetails in rut to help them fill tags will face a much lower-keyed and less helpful situation in muley country. Mule deer are extremely gregarious (far more so than whitetails), milder with each other, less cantankerous with their kind. Often groups that have been hanging together don't even break up for the rut. Bucks are less determinedly territorial. Certainly some serious battles between bucks occur, but many are merely bluffing matches. Discoveries of antler-locked bucks, or bucks killed by antler punctures during breeding season fights, are not as common as with whitetails.

Some scientists believe that not all mule deer bucks of breeding age are interested at the same time. It is rather common to see several bucks pursuing the same doe, without any animosity among them, or even very much excitement evident. I shot a good buck several seasons ago that was with a group of twenty-odd deer, at least three of them eight- and ten-pointers of breeding age, the rest does, fawns, forkhorns. Mule deer are sometimes seen in groups twice that large, and groups of bucks, as many as six to a dozen or more, all mature, commonly hang around together, a distinct difference from the average, far-less-gregarious whitetail habits.

At any rate, I watched these deer for half an hour. One doe definitely was in heat. Each of the older bucks paid minor court. Only one was halfway ardent. There was a bit of running, shoving, posing, but no trouble among the males. The rest of the group paid little attention. The doe in fact was the bold one, the interested buck quite lackadaisical. I tried rattling antlers to see what might happen. Nothing. After experiencing much excitement and drama rattling for whitetails, I've tried it on mule deer numerous times without arousing much interest. Certainly the rut sparks diligent travel in old trophy bucks, without their usual caution, and this may put one into your sights. In general, however, the unwary, rut-crazed buck so easily hung on the whitetail meat pole is seldom seen in muley country.

A curious reaction of muleys, probably indicating both strong curiosity and wilderness naivete, concerns their response to a deer or predator call. A friend in Arizona has demonstrated numerous times how groups of mule deer, including adult bucks, will sometimes all but run over a hunter blowing a predator call. The so-called "deer call" is similar, except lower in pitch, supposedly imitating the *blatt* of a deer.

Undisturbed whitetails will sometimes pause and stare toward a single blatt from a deer call. Anguished blowing on one, or on a predator call, will spook them out of cover. I've used the technique in the south-Texas thorn brush to do just that. Conversely, mule deer will often arise from their beds in midday and move out to see what continued squalling on a deer call is all about. A guide friend constantly uses the method when scouting new territory or when mule deer aren't moving. I've seen a bare slope blossom with half a dozen or more deer popping up from among rocks and bushes to check out the sound. Many will move substantial distances toward the racket. If you intend to try this, first check legality of mouth-blown deer calls where you hunt.

It should be emphasized again that old, trophy mule deer bucks are by no means as easy to collect as some of the traits covered here might make them sound. Nevertheless, they are not especially sly, devious, or crafty. They simply live and stay in, or if necessary move far back into, the wildest, roughest terrain they can find.

Wilderness is always the key for big mule deer. Sure, here and there mule deer in parks or on foothill ranches have become gentle and seem partially to adapt to man's incursions. Not many, though. Look at a state like Pennsylvania, teeming with roughly 12 million people in about 45,000 square miles. The whitetail harvest is annually around 135,000, with another 25,000 or more road kills, and still deer are overabundant. In Montana, more than three times as large, with fewer than a million people, the mule deer harvest averages less than half that. Build a new ski resort in Vermont and presently the whitetails adapt to it. Build one in Colorado and in its vicinity mule deer swiftly begin to disappear.

These animals need space. They evolved from a vast, rugged, remote country and are authentic wilderness creatures, tailored to a complicated land not easy for the hunter to scout and decide where the deer will be, compared to the woodlands where whitetails dwell. Thoroughly understanding the mule deer's personality in relation to its environment, however, makes hunting easier, and increases chances of success.

Using a call for deer is not new. This photo, taken over 30 years ago, shows call maker Murry Burnham experimenting, and bringing in a whitetail buck.

Guide Jim Barbee routinely uses call to bring mule deer out of their beds or cover. He believes they are curious about the sound. This one was, and was collected by hunter client.

CHAPTER 8
CALLING DEER

This whitetail buck was stopped in open while crossing through cover, by a sharp BLATT from a call, giving opportunity for shot.

During recent years the "grunt call" has been much publicized. It's used during the rut, chiefly for whitetails. It mimics the series of grunting sounds a buck sometimes makes while pursuing a doe. Although this call is effective on occasion, it is not the never-fail gadget some advertisers and writers have claimed. Bucks do not make these sounds as commonly as is claimed. Certainly the grunt call is worth trying. But be assured that you might hunt a lifetime without hearing a buck utter the sound. Further, it is effective only during the rut. The following chapter relates incidents and gives material concerning the more general use of calls, both during breeding season and at other times.

Over a period of years I've experimented with deer calls, trying them on both whitetails and mule deer. I learned long ago that the effectiveness of these calls is badly underresearched. Some hunters don't even know there is such a thing. Most who do but who've never tried one scoff at the idea, or are simply uninterested. Opinions among the modest number of hunters with actual experience range from glowingly pro to emphatically con.

The truth about deer calls is this: They do work — sometimes. Murry Burnham, call maker and probably the best known, most experienced, and most expert animal caller around, offers this explanation of their ambiguous status: "A whole lot more deer would be called if a whole lot more hunters regularly used a whole lot more deer calls."

My interest in the subject was sparked long ago. I was hunkered on a ridgeside in the low thornbrush of southern Texas, blowing a predator call for coyotes. That call, as most readers know, mimics the squall of an injured rabbit. Most deer calls are similarly designed, but pitched lower, imitating the bleat of a fawn when gently blown, the raspy blat of an adult deer at more volume, or the anguished bellow of an injured or attacked deer when blasted all-out. Predator calls are commonly used for deer nowadays, and amazingly often with success. Fair imitations of bleats and blats are possible with one.

The Texas brush country is renowned big-whitetail range. As I squalled long and loud, I was surprised to see a trophy buck explode from distant cover, run a few steps, pause to stare, then hightail for the horizon. Within minutes three more deer erupted. It occurred to me that, had the season been open, I could have collected that big buck.

Out of curiosity I began trying both deer and predator calls on whitetails, using varying volume. The standard procedure to attract deer is to look for a place uncrowded by hunters, with the deer un-

Author's son, Terry, demonstrates for the camera the art of ''rattling up'' a whitetail buck during the rut.

Author with good mule deer buck.

Author's son, Mike, checks out a fresh whitetail rub.

Whitetail buck stalked within easy range.

Texas guide, John Finegan, uses leather sling to hurl fist-sized rocks into draws where whitetails may be bedded. This often spooks deer out of dense cover.

Many deer hunters like new snow on the ground for season opening, so fresh deer tracks are easily seen.

Hunters on horseback work a stream course. For either whitetails or mule deer, stream areas are invariably productive.

Whitetail deer are present in diverse terrains, from forest edges and woodlands, from Maine to Washington, to the Appalachians, and deep swamps of the South.

Hunter about to get a shot at a stunning whitetail buck, in the most unusual of whitetail habitats, the cactus and thornbrush of southern Texas near the Mexican border.

disturbed and unaware of the caller's presence. The caller selects a stand in an area where deer may be hidden or moving, a place where he's concealed, but has a good view. Two or three soft, low, questing or pleading bleats are uttered. After several minutes, these are repeated.

A half-hour at each stand is none too much. Perseverance, all successful call users agree, is important. Occasionally a deer may rush in. More often the animals will sneak, unseen, not showing themselves for some minutes. Sparse calling is recommended. If no deer shows, occasionally a loud blat or two may get results. Moves between stands should be far enough to be outside hearing range.

Summer practice results generally shouldn't be equated with calling during deer season. Does come readily, I discovered, when fawns are small. They responded to the quiet bleat less often in fall. Bucks seldom showed. However, I did manage — and have since repeated it quite often — to stop a moving buck in an opening within shooting range by uttering a sharp blat. Occasionally this is a tag filler, when either stand or still hunting.

To illustrate how well it can work, Peter Barrett, then fishing editor of *Field & Stream*, and I once spent several days shooting whitetail photos on the YO Ranch in Texas. We cruised ranch roads and when we spotted a deer in cover, we stopped and blew the call. We enticed numerous bucks into openings. They'd stop, peer, looking alert, posing for us. Peter even tried a squawk now and then on a pheasant call. Same result. Repetition however, quickly spooked them. I've used this negative response to my benefit by repeatedly blowing loud deer-call blatts and predator call squalls to flush whitetail bucks from cover. Several whitetail guides I know habitually do this to chouse whitetails out for their hunters.

Overall, however, reactions of whitetails are erratic. You'd best be prepared for the unexpected. Some even come running to high-decibel, anguished predator calling, though the consensus of hunters and call makers throughout the country who've used deer calls is that more whitetails are flushed than attracted, and that more does by far than bucks respond positively. For instance, one Oklahoma hunter, using a predator call for bobcats, coyotes, and foxes, has unintentionally brought in sixty-five does. It all adds up to the conclusion that a great deal about deer calling may still need to be learned.

I've discovered that numerous unpublicized hunters who've long used calls routinely consider success a foregone conclusion. One Georgian wrote that for twenty years he and his father have been complaining that the call they use makes their hunts too short! Such successes aren't regional. They occur in virtually every whitetail state. A Maryland hunter ordered a call by mail, eagerly tested it in the backyard of his country home, and drew in the biggest buck he'd ever seen. A North Dakota hunter was popeyed when his predator call brought a big whitetail buck on the run. In Massachusetts, a skeptical deer caller had his hackles raised when a buck raced in, "madder than hell." In New York State one enthusiast has brought in and bagged bucks several seasons running. The majority who've been able to *attract* whitetails believe the responses are unpredictable, individual, and due mostly to curiosity mingled with uncertainty.

The reactions of mule deer are decidedly different — far more positive and predictable. I was with a game department friend in Arizona one fall who demonstrated. He blew a predator call and I thought we were going to get run over. Both bucks and does came running, extremely agitated. For some seasons now I have hunted mule deer each fall with Jim Barbee, a West Texas guide. His deer call is as much a part of standard equipment as his binocular and rifle.

Barbee uses it chiefly to locate mule deer. I've walked with him many times to the side of a ridge overlooking a broad canyon, where we'd thoroughly glass the undisturbed area. Not a deer. Then he'd start blowing. Within a few minutes there'd be deer, both bucks and does, rising from beds or hiding places, staring.

One midday Barbee and I sat on the edge of a high mesa glassing down into shadowed areas of a vast slope and valley of intricate rock patterns laced with brush and scattered trees. He worked the call with loud intermittent blasts for 10 minutes. One by one we saw scattered deer arise and move to look up. We had five excellent bucks in sight at one time. Finally they all became too disturbed, and ran. On another occasion, after we called for a few minutes from a high rock perch above a steep, narrow, wooded canyon, deer began appearing. Presently we looked down upon a string of ten mule deer, eight does and two bucks, coming toward us single file, ears cocked. The caravan stopped when the lead animal was possibly 75 yards distant. At last too much was too much and they all fled.

The experience of Major L. Boddicker of Rocky Mt. Wildlife Products, who markets and uses a predator call, is that mule deer, even does and fawns, often come in "with very hostile attitudes, snorting, stamping their feet, shaking their heads, ears forward, hair on end.

On two occasions one lead doe actually made an attempt to hit me with her front feet," Boddicker says.

He tells also of being present, along with a Nebraska Game Department employee, when a partner called and a *herd* of mule deer "came literally thundering in and chased him up a tree, circling for several minutes before leaving."

For years Murry and Winston Burnham successfully used calls for mule deer in the Rockies. I hunted one fall with them in Colorado when every now and then a buck raised our hair, running at us. James Olt, of the venerable Olt Co. in Illinois, tells of a predator-calling trip one time near Gillette, Wyoming, when mule deer repeatedly almost ran them down at night. "We'd hear them pounding in, even coming from downwind, right into our scent and the predator light. We'd switch off the light and they'd clatter up within 25 yards. Why they came in such a rush, I have no idea. Curiosity?" Yet Jim Olt and Murry Burnham admit there are times when mule deer pay no attention to deer or predator calls, and they don't know why that happens, either.

Blacktail deer, especially the Sitka, are possibly the most responsive — or else it's simply that the calls have been used on them more, since for many years calling has been a standard hunting method in Alaska. Some callers use loud bleats, presumably imitating the distress squalls of a fawn or doe. Some blow a very soft, drawn-out *baaaa*. Both bring Sitka deer out of dense cover, sometimes in a rush, but often sneaking, taking some minutes to appear. Predator calls are used also. I was told by one Alaskan correspondent that he uses with startling success a quail call from the Lower 48, blown with a full-volume, high-pitched squeal.

Lohman Mfg. Co., old-line call makers located in Neosho, Missouri, told me that for some years they had orders "by the gross" from retailers in Alaska for a quail call they designed originally for California valley quail. They discovered these were being used for Sitka blacktails. They then switched to making an Alaskan deer call specifically for that purpose. It is also used effectively, along with a standard deer call Lohman builds, in the lower states. Successful blacktail callers agree that the hunter must not be seen or scented; that, as with other deer, calm days are best; and, finally, that responses are most numerous under uncrowded conditions.

Attempts to call deer are by no means modern. American Indians made sounds by mouth, or blew on a grass blade held between the thumbs. Ojibways fashioned a series of wooden cones with a reed inside, and Northwestern tribes made somewhat similar calls. Even modern deer calls have been around awhile. The first one, as nearly as I can tell, was patented and marketed nationally back in the 1940s by outdoor writer Arthur H. Carhart.

Possibly the most unusual approach was conceived years ago by Jack Lohman, who founded the Lohman Mfg. Co. As early as the 1950s he was making a deer "snort" call for friends. These were used when prowling or stalking, to answer a deer that uttered the sound when alerted. Some hunters like to believe it is the bucks that make this sound. Actually it's more likely to be a doe. The sound is an indication that the deer is disturbed, but puzzled. It's not a nasal snort as most suppose. I've observed deer numerous times at close range as they "blow." Air is expelled through the nearly closed mouth with such force that, after a few repetitions, white froth forms on the lips.

The claim is made for the "snort" call Lohman now markets that bucks in rut will run toward the sound, and "snorting" deer will have fears allayed, believing another deer is nearby. Not everyone agrees. When deer — chiefly whitetails — blow that way, it signals emphatic uneasiness. When they continue intermittently, then let fly a series of fast, short "snorts," you can bet they're running. Guide John Finegan in Texas imitates by mouth the blowing sound to flush hiding whitetails from thickets.

Sounds that appeal to deer have always been the puzzler for call inventors. Deer aren't gregarious, and most important, they aren't vocal. In fact, their limited vocabulary is seldom heard by hunters. Aside from the "snort" of a disturbed deer, or, rarely, the grunt of a buck pursuing a doe, few have ever heard a deer make a sound. In fifty years of deer hunting, I've only once heard a fawn bleating as it wandered, probably seeking its mother. On two occasions I watched and heard a doe utter a low blat. Twice I've heard loud, gutteral, rasping squalls; one came from a wounded buck, the other from a doe caught by stray dogs.

All attempts to appeal to deer by calls have been based on vocal sounds they utter only infrequently, so it is remarkable that the scheme works at all. But the fact is that calls *do* call deer. Certainly they're no infallible answer to putting venison on the pole, but the hunter who scoffs is missing a chance at least to improve the odds slightly. To paraphrase Murry Burnham's claim, it's a cinch more deer would be called if more hunters decided deer calls were worth at least a toot.

Author's son, Mike, hurries to whitetail buck he'd shot that passed unconcerned within short range while pursuing doe.

Whitetail bucks sometimes battle viciously during rut like these two. Mule deer are less pugnacious.

CHAPTER 9

THE RUT

Whitetail buck follows scent of doe. They sometimes become so addled they pay no attention to nearby hunters.

Early in my deer hunting experience an incident occurred that impressed upon me the amazing changes the period of the rut brings temporarily to the lives of deer, and how important it can be to the success of hunting. The incident took place in northern Michigan on a
still, cold November morning when crusty snow crackled underfoot.
I was planning to sit on an ancient pine stump half a mile from camp,
and was hurrying at dawn through dense poplar and conifer forest, making no attempt to walk quietly because it wasn't possible. Along my
way was a small opening.

As I came into it, gun slung, hands in coat pockets, a doe glided
across from about 2 o'clock on my right. I stopped spang in the open.
She stopped off to my left, barely 50 yards, and looked behind, flopping her ears that way. Astonishingly, she seemed wholly unaware of
me.

Then I heard a series of deep, gutteral grunts: *arghh — arghh —
arghh* — uttered by an eight-point buck that now appeared, nose to
the snow, following the doe's track. Few hunters to whom I've talked
over the intervening forty years have ever heard this sound. I have on
only a few occasions. Deer are not very vocal creatures. But once heard,
this sound is not easily forgotten. Knowledge of it is an important oddment of rut-season lore. It means a buck is nearby, following a doe,
and probably an easy mark.

The doe coquettishly wheeled away into cover to the left. Uttering those odd grunts again, the buck came on. Slowly I tried to get
my rifle in hand. The buck, not forty steps out front, became aware,
turned, and stopped, facing me, not a twig between us.

His stance and expression were as if he were trying to force his
senses back, not very successfully, from some dream world. What happened then seemed unbelievable, but it made such an impression that
I've been prepared ever since, and have taken a number of desire-addled
bucks which performed just as preposterously. Instead of reacting to
me, the buck seemed to dismiss me as only some hazily registered
interruption to romance, and he turned, lowered his head to pick up
the doe's track scent again, and was gone into cover along her trail
before I got my wits in gear.

What "the rut" means to most deer hunters is that two- or three-
week period when the breeding season is at its peak. That by no means
covers the entire breeding season, which begins earlier and ends much
later, but it is the time when most activity occurs. It is therefore the
period when competition among bucks for the favor of does is at its

highest, and when hunters who are informed about the drastic changes in deer lives at that time have the most chances of finding even large, old bucks making fatal errors.

What is not always understood by hunters is that the rut is not launched because the bucks, as it's said, "start running." It is the does that determine when breeding will begin. The bucks are simply ready and restlessly waiting. The amount of light available is the basic spark for conditioning both bucks and does for breeding. In fall, shorter days and less light induce hormone flows that govern the animals' sexual lives. Interestingly, deer kept in darkened pens and exposed to less than normal daylight can be induced to breed earlier than they normally would.

As the rut approaches, bucks begin mock battles with small trees and bushes, making so-called rubs on the bark. Those found early in fall or in late summer are made by bucks scrubbing off antler velvet. The important rubs for hunters to locate are made just prior to and during the rut. They are energetic, even vicious attacks, often shredding and killing small trees. Numerous fresh rubs in an area at this time indicate that a buck dwells here. It's important for a hunter to realize that in any given area bucks prefer certain kinds of saplings for mock battles. Learning which species are preferred on your own hunting ground will help you find the deer.

The first buck rubs I discovered were in northern Michigan, where the animals mostly used small balsams. I remember how proud I was of my deer lore when, after locating a scattering of balsam rubs within an expanse of perhaps 50 acres, I sat in a small opening on opening morning and killed a buck. The incident was wryly comic, because I actually heard the buck before I saw it — fighting a witchhazel clump!

Many bucks, especially larger ones, begin to show swelled necks in fall. Several theories have been concocted about this phenomenon, but the careful observer should note that not all bucks are affected. Some researchers believe the swelling may be caused by a hormone. Others claim that the heavy-antlered, most vigorous bucks develop this change because of added antler weight, which is substantial, plus incessant exercise of neck muscles during mock fights with saplings, and some actual battles with other bucks. Seldom does one see a thin- or small-antlered buck with a swollen neck.

Although some does develop breeding capability as young as six or eight months, bucks are unable to breed until their second fall, when they are long yearlings, around eighteen months old. These young bucks during their first rut are easy pickin's for a hunter who is aware of their gullibility.

To both deer and hunters, the most important sign made during the rut is the scrape of the buck. Scrapes are pawed-out places in soft earth, 2 or 3 feet long and perhaps 18 inches wide, in which a buck urinates. During this period the tarsal gland on the inside of each hind leg — of both sexes — oozes and is wet with a smelly secretion.

Invariably a scrape is made where a branch or bush overhangs. The first high deer stand I was ever in, in Texas, overlooked a fresh scrape made by a buck. The seat was in a tree, and I watched the buck that visited the scrape but didn't shoot because this was a valuable opportunity to observe his routine. He'd reach up and tickle his antler tips against the overhanging branch, nibble at its twigs and leaves, and rub his face against them. Some scientists claim the preorbital glands, near the inside corner of each eye, secrete a substance that is rubbed onto bushes and twigs to mark out a buck's breeding territory, and on branches overhanging a scrape. Others deny that this is true.

Whichever is correct, this buck — and others I've watched — did appear to rub leaves and twigs into the eye corners. Not long after the buck left the scrape, a doe moved past my stand, went to the scrape, sniffed, and also urinated in it. Does visit buck scrapes to alert the bucks that they are available. A buck makes several scrapes around his territory.

Whether or not these mark off an inviolate breeding territory is debated among researchers and practiced observers. Even buck fights, some of them vicious, may not be caused by territoriality. I have taken a stand near a scrape and rattled up as many as four different bucks, each of which saw at least one of the others, but none of which attempted to fight. I have seen a big buck move threateningly toward a young one, but the youngster didn't wait to protest.

Deer do not form harems, like elk, although some observers claim mule deer do. Mule deer are much more gregarious, placid, less aggressive than whitetails. These habits may create an erroneous impression of harem gathering. I have watched mule deer many seasons, with some breeding in progress each year. The endless chases on which whitetail does lead bucks do not seem at all common among mule deer. I've watched a buck — sometimes several — with a group of does, intermittently chasing and circling a particular doe that apparently was ready to be bred. Because there was no long chase, it would be easy to assume the other mule deer does milling around were a harem. They paid no attention, however, and doubtless were simply part of the gregarious group.

Because of the brief twenty-four hour period each doe is in breeding condition, the rut is a frenzied period for the bucks, and this of course is why they are so vulnerable. A doe baits the interest of a buck, who pursues her. Round and round she leads him, over a ridge and back, over two more and around. She pauses to look back, flopping her ears toward him. He trails, nose to the ground like a hound, or neck thrust out low and straight. It is easy to understand how a hunter may take advantage of such a situation. Deer at this time put aside caution and wariness, paying little attention to possible dangers. Actions of the doe are a giveaway to any observant hunter, often before the buck is seen.

Incidentally, I have observed two interesting buck habits of importance to hunters that I've never seen mentioned anywhere. One is that a whitetail buck making an all-out chase after a fast-moving doe commonly runs with his tail straight out behind.

The other curious habit is the way a buck sometimes charges at a doe, head low, exactly as if he intends to gore her, stopping barely short. As he runs, he slams each hoof down hard, with a flop of the ankle joint at the same instant, to make a curious clicking sound. The effect is an almost simultaneous whack of hoof and click of joint, in running rhythm. If the ground is reasonably bare, and the deer unseen, you can sometimes hear this sound and instantly know what's going on.

A buck chasing a doe may stay constantly with her for a couple of days. Other bucks may interfere, with or without battles occurring. Most buck battles are sparked when super-aggressive bucks happen upon one another. Usually there's little harm. Occasionally, however, a "mad" buck, driven to a frenzy of desire, gores another, and there are authenticated instances of does that teased a temperamental buck too long having been furiously gored to death.

A substantial number of does fail to breed, or else do not conceive, during the first main fall breeding period. These will be in condition again twenty-eight days later, and any that fail that time will have a final third period in another twenty-eight days. Thus there are minor breeding periods, or ruts, much later than the fall peak. Many hunters are unaware of this activity, believing the breeding season is over after the main frenzy.

One fall I was visiting a ranch near my home in early September and the owner, who is an expert at rattling-up bucks, decided out of curiosity to see if he could arouse any action. We took a stand, well hidden, and he had a buck coming in toward us in a few minutes. Obviously this buck was already becoming incautious, although the main rut would not occur for two more months.

I was on the same ranch in early January after deer season had closed, and saw a buck chasing a doe. I stopped my vehicle and watched the animals for 10 minutes as they circled round and round the territory. Without question this was a doe that had failed to breed earlier. There were four whole months between the two occurrences. A hunter who knows when the peak is in his region should be sure to mark the dates and watch closely a month later, if the season is open, and even two months, if deer are still legal. Also, if there is an early season, as there often is for archers, it may pay to try rattling, or watching for "rutty" bucks. The bucks are certain to be eager for the breeding season to begin, restless, and some may be especially gullible.

During the rut peak period particularly, the hunter who patiently searches for scrapes and stakes one out will almost certainly bag a buck. This period is also the best of the season for collecting a big deer. Everyone knows that the old buster bucks haven't made many mistakes in keeping their private lives private, or they wouldn't be old buster bucks. But when lovelight glazes their eyes they are so single-minded of purpose that they seem to put aside all caution. The majority of trophy-sized whitetails I've killed were taken during the rut.

Knowing the general timing in his area of the main rut is vital to the hunter who schemes to use it to advantage. It varies with climate and latitude. In southern Alaska the Sitka blacktail may breed as early as August. The farther north, also, the more distinct and brief the rut period generally is. The average peak across the Northern contiguous states is around the middle of November. There are minor local variations between whitetails and mule deer in places because of altitude differences, which translate to different seasons.

Curiously, the peak of the rut changes only slightly from the Northern states down into the upper South. But somewhere a vague line of latitude seems to be drawn below which emphatic differences do occur. In southern Florida and on the Keys, studies have indicated lack of a precisely defined breeding season. Where I live in central Texas, peak is roughly early to mid-November. But 200 miles south along the Mexican border it occurs later, from mid-December into

January. The same situation occurs with the Coues deer in Arizona and Mexico. Breeding peaks in January. In the tropics, breeding season has no sharp definition. Fawns are seen at almost any time of year.

Scientists do concede that though the amount of light, the latitude, and the general seasonal temperatures at various latitudes are the important basics in manipulating the rut, a quick drop in temperature from unseasonably warm or mild weather to a sudden cool or cold interlude triggers seething activity among deer that have been lackadaisical about breeding. Any hunter who has waited for a cold snap, especially in Southern areas, to "set the bucks to running" will heartily agree.

I recall numerous instances in southern Texas when deer season was hot, and we'd hunt early and late without seeing bucks. One night I especially remember when everyone in camp went to bed without covers, all camp-house windows flung wide. The weather was still and hot.

About 4 A.M. a first small puff of breeze moved the curtains. Ten minutes later a norther was whistling in as they can only whistle in Texas. Temperature dropped swiftly. We were all awake and eager, everyone predicting what was going to happen. At daylight the temperature had dropped 30 degrees. We were out hunting, and bucks seemed to pop out of the ground, several chasing does. I've seen the same thing in south Texas when the temperature dropped only slightly — a minor front moving in and the temperature lowering not more than 5 or 10 degrees.

A most important factor hunters seldom consider in regard to the amount of rut activity they observe is the matter of herd balance or imbalance. Countless sex-ratio studies over many years have shown that at birth there are very slightly more male than female fawns, on the average around 51 percent. In areas where bucks are incessantly hunted, and especially where two or more per season may be killed, herds may become badly imbalanced, with far too many does. Restrictions on doe killing, and attitudes against it, further complicate matters.

A single buck may service anywhere from half a dozen to twenty or more does. But if there are not enough bucks to find and have time to breed all the does, a much more sustained but far less frenzied rut will occur. There is then little severe competition among bucks, and many does are not bred until their third — very late — period, and many may go barren.

A competitive rut, which is high drama for hunters, usually indicates a well-managed — that is, a sexually well-balanced — deer herd. And by proper management most biologists mean a sex ratio of adult deer of roughly one to one. From this a curious paradox arises: If you want to enjoy the thrills and excitement of watching the love-addled antics of numerous heavy-antlered competitive bucks during the fall rut, you have to do your share in harvesting the surplus does!

Author uses antler tines to claw rough tree bark, part of the antler rattling routine to simulate fighting buck sounds.

Author brings buck close by rattling antlers.

CHAPTER 10
RATTLE UP A BUCK

Hunter, with rattling antlers hung over shoulder, moves in on downed buck that came to the ruse.

The ten-point whitetail buck had come on the run, nostrils flared, eyes wild, straight at us, appearing ready to fight. It had in fact skidded to a stop within a mere fifteen feet of where the two of us hunched in a cedar thicket. Not a shot was fired.

I hadn't intended to shoot anyway. I had in tow a visiting deer hunter from Wisconsin. I had taken him to my own modest-sized Texas ranch to try to get him a buck by "rattling it up" during the rut. Rattling means clashing together a pair of deer antlers individually sawed from the skull of a previous season's kill to simulate two bucks fighting.

He had told me suspiciously and emphatically that I was pulling his leg. It was ridiculous to suppose such a thing could be done. This, he inferred, was just one more instance of wind flowing through a Texan. Several years ago I had rattled up 52 bucks into camera range during an especially concentrated rut in 10 days of producing a TV film for a firearms manufacturer. And I had brought in a good many more before and since, as well as watching others do likewise.

Probably letting a dead-to-rights ten like that get away isn't funny. But as the buck plunged all-out toward us, I had expected my hunter to shoot. Instead, when the animal appeared about to crash at full speed into the thicket with us, he had hollered, "Look out!" and had crashed out the other side. Now he returned sheepishly, a silly small grin creasing his face, saying, "So okay, I still don't believe it!"

The statement was a neat wrap-up of why the sensationally dramatic practice of rattling for whitetails is not practiced more throughout the nation. Except for a handful of Texans, and a handful of openminded souls elsewhere who have seen it done or done it, *nobody* believes it, so nobody tries it. Thus many hunters miss one of the greatest thrills in deer hunting, and just maybe go deerless when they might collect a buster.

Rattling up whitetails, *which is successful only during the rut*, supposedly originated many years ago in the Mexican border region of southern Texas, in the so-called Brush Country. This vast expanse of cactus and thornbrush contains a substantial population of outsized whitetails. All but a couple of the Texas record-book whitetails have come out of the Brush Country. The method is supposed to have originated because the cover is so dense it was about the only way to get a buck up close, and visible, and somehow, old timers discovered the trick.

Years ago, I remember hearing on a trip to Texas that rattling would not work anywhere else, even within the state. Later, when we came to live permanently in Texas, in the live oak and cedar of the Hill Country some 200 miles north of the border brush, Charlie Schreiner, owner of the YO Ranch renowned nationwide for its hunting, was already rattling up bucks by the swarm.

It was from Charlie that I first learned the technique. I recall vividly with some amusement the frosty, still dawn when he first demonstrated it for me. While I smirked patronizingly at his racket and ritual, he brought an eight-pointer up literally within six feet. It stared at us, whirled and ran off, but when Charlie tickled the antlers gently again, the rut-addled buck came right back. Like my Wisconsin hunter, I didn't shoot either. I was utterly flabbergasted.

The extension of rattling success up into central Texas, it was said, was because deer were so abundant in the Hill Country. This made no sense. Competition for does was not stiff. Does were and are so over-abundant in the Hill Country that except for the natural instinct bucks need not compete at all. And down in the border brush where the method originated, although deer were present in fair numbers, the population is not really high. When Charlie Schreiner first began experimenting with rattling on his YO Ranch in central Texas, there was an awesome overpopulation of deer and no competition for does necessary — and still the bucks would all but run over you when you rattled.

The plain fact is, rattling will work anywhere if the season falls during the rut, which it does in a majority of states. Regardless of the level of deer population, under proper conditions, bucks within hearing will respond. The sound carries surprisingly far, especially on those still, crisp dawns when rattling is most successful. Obviously, there may be times when a buck, perhaps sated, or maybe spooked by too many hunters in the woods, or for some reason suspicious, won't come to the sound. You shouldn't expect magic every time. But it's a sure bet no buck will come if you don't try it. And certainly, if rattling improves your chances even as little as 10 percent, (I'll bet on 50 percent) it's worth fooling with. I can promise one thing, once you've seen a buck come to rattled antlers, you'll be hooked for the remainder of your hunting life.

A few years ago in a book of mine I covered whitetail rattling, and received mail from a wide area, from hunters who'd been successful rattling. One man in Pennsylvania, as I recall, had been rattling — not for hunting but just for fun — over a period of a decade, and had logged over 100 bucks that came in. There were other successful rattlers who wrote from Minnesota, North Dakota, Nebraska, a couple of New England states, Missouri, and Oklahoma.

If you want to try rattling, here are the simple steps for preparing a proper set of antlers:

1. Select a head of 8 or 10 points. I use 8.
2. Avoid very light, extra-heavy or weathered antlers.
3. Saw each antler from the skull below the burl.
4. Saw off the brow tines. They'll hurt your hands.
5. Saw off any nubbins or "almost" points. They'll be in the way.
6. If points are extra sharp, saw off tips to blunt them.
7. File smooth all saw cuts.
8. Tie a thong between antlers, above burl, for easy carrying.

There is no cut and dried rattling routine. You can simply "rattle," but here's how mine generally goes.

1. Select a stand where you can sit, well hidden but able to see into an opening of modest size surrounded by good cover.
2. Try for one (not absolutely necessary) that has within reach: A-a thick bush; B-a rough-barked tree; C-a patch of gravel or small stones.
3. Grasp antlers by bases, left in left hand, right in right hand, beam curves just as they were on head.
4. Bring them smartly together, meshing tines naturally with a sharp crack.
5. Holding antlers in that position, rattle the tines once or twice, then twist together to make grating sound.
6. Whack and claw bush with one or both antlers, several blows.
7. Rake tines of one antler down rough bark of tree.
8. Rake tines of one antler across gravel or stones.
9. Rattle and clash once more.
10. Wait fifteen to thirty seconds, then repeat or vary at will.
11. Stay on one stand at least half an hour, intermittently rattling, with longer pauses between.
12. If buck appears distantly, undecided, rattle very gently, "tickling" tines together. Rake gravel gently.
13. An effective variation in this routine to intersperse: turn antlers over and pound on turf two or three times to imitate stomping feet.
14. When you move to a new stand, move at least a half mile.

The basis for the rattling theory is simple. Whitetail bucks commonly battle during breeding season. Each makes rubs on saplings prior to the rut, then later stakes out his territory with scrapes — shallow diggings of the front hoofs in which the animal urinates to authenticate its presence. A buck makes several scrapes outlining its home territory boundaries. Bucks then raid each other's territories, seeking does. Whitetails do not form harems, like elk, but will breed any available doe ready to be serviced. Each doe is in heat for only roughly 24 hours. Thus, although all are not in heat at once, the competition at rut peak among bucks is often severe.

Depending upon latitude, the rut begins anywhere from late September on through October and November. It may run into January in the south. Generally, mid-Oct. to end of Nov. catches the peak almost anywhere, as well as most deer seasons.

When a buck discovers another in his domain or during his foray into another's, a fight usually occurs, whether or not either is with a doe. Rattling simply simulates the sounds of such a battle. I always check first for several rubbed saplings, and then look for scrapes. The two add up to proof positive that a buck is "at home" here, and probably operating within a fairly small area, a half square mile or less. It's just a matter of careful and quiet stand selection, particularly near fresh rubs and scrapes, until rattling will bring him around with fire in his eye.

Bucks don't always come barreling in. When one does, he's easy pickin's. However, I've often had one circle suspiciously. If there are a few bushes or a tree or two in the opening you're watching, be assured such a buck will use them to screen himself. I've also had them come pussyfooting in with great stealth. This gent's scheme is to run off with a doe while the fight progresses. Sometimes a buck will startle you witless, coming from behind. I've had one I never knew was there snort and turn wrong side out within a yard of my back when it got my scent. That, I'll guarantee, will raise your hackles!

Spikes are often comics, a bit like teenage lovers, sort of bumbly, and naive. A couple of years ago I sat in plain sight of any deer that came close. A spike larruped in, looked at me, switched its tail, wheeled away. I gently rattled, very quietly, just the antler tips. Back it came, staring and twitching.

You always should keep intent watch on a young buck. Wherever it looks, you look. It doesn't want trouble from a big buck, and it will spot one coming, flick its ears and finally mince away. It is not uncommon where deer are abundant to bring in more than one. During production of the TV film I mentioned earlier, I had four come in on two different occasions to a stand, all warily watching each other.

Dawn, as noted, is the prime time. Still, cold mornings are best. Sound carries well and no breeze gives you away. Stay with it until at least 9:30 a.m. Windy days are poor. A strong wind makes deer nervous, even during rut. Any noticeable breeze will cause incoming bucks to circle, to get the wind on your position. This is instinctive. A rule when any breeze is moving is to sit either facing it and watching chiefly both right and left, or else to sit with it directly on one shoulder or the other, and keep watch straight ahead and to the side into the wind.

If you simply enjoy the rattling idea, don't give up entirely in the middle of the day, but always stay on a stand longer then. I once spent an hour fiddling with a buck that I saw distantly arise from its bed. It was curious but really not very interested. Yet, at last, after I'd been still a long time then cranked up again, it couldn't resist. It walked slowly out into the open to check what was going on.

During the peak of the rut, the couple of weeks when the most does are bred, a buck is more likely to race in at the first rattle. Earlier or later it may take more time. Make a rule to stay longer on a stand where deer are abundant. A raiding buck or several may come into hearing range. Where deer are scarce, move on if you don't get action in twenty minutes and keep moving, covering a lot of territory.

I mentioned selecting a stand overlooking a small opening. Whitetails seldom will come across a broad open valley. They love to forage in, and chase does round and round through breaks of modest expanse inside cover. Look for the rubs, then the scrapes, then a nearby small open area within cover, anywhere from fifty to a hundred yards in longest dimension. If it has a few scattered bushes, so much the better. One immense advantage of these snug havens is that the buck has no chance to see you — until you see him well within range.

A question that always arises is: what about mule deer? Mule deer are by no means as aggressive during the rut as whitetails are. Serious battles are fewer. To date I have not been able to bring in mule deer. I don't intend to cross them off. They've been tried very little. But I already know how gullible the whitetail is to this unusual approach.

Indeed, if you'll lay aside skepticism, give rattling an open-minded try during the rut, and persist in the endeavor even though you may not have lightning strike the first time out, one will get you ten that sooner or later you'll join the believers — and probably shake and forget to shoot during your conversion!

Best stance for a buck you decide to shoot is broadside, offering either neck or rib placement.

This deer running straight away offers no proper placement. You should hold fire.

CHAPTER 11
DISCIPLINING YOUR SHOT
PLACEMENTS

This hunter has a precarious shot. It must be carefully placed in chest or very close behind shoulder. Neither choice is recommended.

The term "meat hunter," as most deer hunters are aware, is no compliment. During my early days of whitetail hunting, I hunted several times with an old gentleman who was known throughout the region as one of those. I asked him one time if that didn't irritate him.

"No," he replied. "I consider it a compliment. The hunter who thinks always about the meat has the sportiest hunting of all."

At the time I wasn't sure what he meant. As the seasons passed, and I began to fit the mold more and more myself, I began to understand. Far too many whitetail hunters, I discovered, were so eager to put a deer on the ground — any deer — that they practiced no restraint whatever. They accepted meat-ruining shots and impossible running shots. Any place you could hit a deer was good enough.

The worst example I can recall occurred one season on a Texas ranch when I was guided the first morning by a ranch hand who'd also been assigned another hunter, a stranger to me. To be polite, I suggested he be the first shooter. Presently a forkhorn ran up a ridge and stopped momentarily to stare. The guide told the hunter it was too small. The buck ran and the hunter started shooting anyway. He hit a haunch. The deer hesitated. He shot again. Before he quit he had put five shots into it.

As we walked to it, the hunter seemed excited and pleased with his prowess. The cowboy looked at the deer, then squirted a stream of snuff juice within an inch of the hunter's boots. With obvious disgust he said, "I'm not even gonna clean it. I'm gonna put it just as is into a bag for you, and label it venison hamburg with the hair on!"

I was remembering the old meat hunter of my early experiences. He claimed he'd never wounded or lost a deer, that he never shot at a running deer, that he accepted only shots that *he* wanted, not any one a deer happened to present to him. He said he always passed up deer until he saw one either with large antlers, or in perfect physical condition, or both.

"That's how old time market hunters did it," he told me. "They wanted the best meat and didn't want to ruin any of it. You know, that's real sport hunting, and the curious part is, the meat hunter shots are the only ones that put a deer down for sure, *right now*."

When you ponder this gentleman's hunting philosophy, you realize that meat hunting for whitetails, viewed from that angle, is the highest challenge. You select an animal you really want, either for its trophy antlers or exceptional meat, or both. You pass up deer, sometimes for a whole season, and may wind up with unfilled tag. I realize this is difficult. It requires total restraint. You also accept only the shots you decide you can make, those that ruin as little meat as possible and are the most certainly lethal.

One of the best whitetail bucks I ever failed to collect stood on a ranch tank dam down near the Mexican border in Texas, at possibly 300 yards. I had a good rest atop a fencepost. The deer stood at a three-quarter rear-on angle. I could see the angled right side, but at that range trying to place a bullet in the neck was impossible, and a lung shot most precarious. Given the shallow angle, a paunch hit might result. I wanted that buck. I said to it, "Turn broadside and I'll try." The buck walked on, keeping the same angle.

A friend who was with me said, "That was dumb. You may not get another chance all season at one that good."

My heart was still pounding. I said, "I thought it was as sporty as it comes." A meat-hunter friend expresses it better. He claims there's more drama and pride in an unfilled tag that results from being choosy than in ten so-so bucks impetuously put on the ground.

The so-called "meat-hunter" shot placements are rather limited. The commonly used broadside shoulder shot, for example, is frowned upon by the meat hunter. It usually ruins one shoulder, and on small deer especially, may ruin or bloody the other. The spine shot, certainly lethal, is another meat-hunter no-no. Made from broadside, the loin is destroyed, and if attempted from the rear, portions of the upper hams also may be ruined.

Obviously the paunch area is to be scrupulously avoided. This leaves very little of the whole deer to be shot at. Further, placement must be precise, which makes these the most difficult but sportiest shots at whitetails. Additionally, the deer must stand just so. Waiting for one to do so, or not do so, wraps up the whole meaning of hunter restraint, hunter excitement, and suspended drama.

Bob Brister once wrote of the advice of a rancher with whom he hunted whitetails. The front half of the deer, he said, is where you kill it. The rear half is where you wound it. My early-day mentor told me, "There are really only three acceptable meat-hunter shots: the neck; the lungs; the heart."

These destroy very little desirable meat. Only the expert and unflappable shooters, however, should try neck shots. Excitable nimrods who wave their rifle barrels, and so-so shooters who too often aim here and hit there may strike the jaw or windpipe, wounding and probably losing the animal. The average hunter's best bet is the lung shot. It should be placed from broadside, high in the ribs but well below the backbone. Some deer may run a short distance, although many are instantly downed.

The heart shot is tricky, because the heart lies very low — lower than many hunters realize — along the brisket. It is also partially protected by the forelegs and shoulders when a deer stands straight. Inept placement may mean a broken foreleg or a paunch-shot animal, and perhaps a lost one. Also, heart-shot deer very often make a desperate run before giving out, and in this way are lost for good.

One year I did a survey of ten top whitetail states, asking deer-management biologists about the makeup of the annual kill. All told, antlerless deer were about 30 percent. Spikes, forkhorns, and bucks with no more than six points were roughly 65 percent. This left 5 percent for larger-antlered bucks, and of those, authentic trophies and record-book entries were only a fraction of the total.

When I asked at several locker plants about attitudes toward meat, the butchers just shook their heads. One said, "Most deer brought in are worthless as trophies, and an astonishing percentage are shot up so bad they're almost worthless for meat, too."

I thought about that hunter who had shot the little buck five times. He didn't have a trophy deer. He didn't have meat worth hauling home. He hadn't had a worthwhile hunting experience. One meat-hunter friend told me last season, as we watched hunters unloading a pickup of so-so bucks at a locker plant, "There's no reason to shoot the average buck *except* for the venison. So if you pick a scrawny animal and blow the heck out of it to boot, you haven't got your money's worth either in sport or meat."

The meat hunter bones up on how to select a *good* deer, and in lieu of massive antlers, becomes extremely selective about physical condition. How do you judge whitetails on the hoof? It's not as difficult as it might seem. First of all, you should understand that the whitetail is an extremely nervous animal, not placid like its mule deer relative. Feeding, it constantly twitches and jerks its head erect to stare or listen.

I've watched whitetails that were bedded and chewing their cud. They never seem to drowse or settle down. Ears flop this way and that. Eyes are always intently staring. It is obvious that this deer species never will be as fat as big-game animals that are not so suspicious and jumpy. A "fat" whitetail compared to a fat mule deer is only larded so-so.

Nevertheless, whitetails on the hoof readily indicate by various physical attributes what their condition is. Just as there are some whitetails with trophy antlers, there are some that are meat trophies. Judgment begins with an evaluation of the kind of year it has been for the deer. If there have been rains, and good crops of deer forage such as acorns, most of the healthy deer will be fat. If there has been drought and meager forage, then only the most vigorous animals will show prime condition. Then you have to be more selective than ever.

One year on our own ranch we'd had fair rains, but only a middling acorn crop. I hunted all season without seeing a buck that suited me. Meanwhile, I had spotted a certain doe that was round as a butterball. Late in the season I decided to settle on meat alone. That doe proved to be nicely padded with fat and a prime choice.

Judging the physical condition of a whitetail is not just a matter of picking out one that "looks fat." A friend who is strictly a meat hunter says, "I use a binocular and really study each deer. In dim light, or when you're excited about a certain deer's size, it's easy to misjudge. If it appears the deer will move into better light, I wait on it. Any deer on which I can see rib outlines high on the sides, I pass up — unless it's a monster buck I want.

Cattlemen will tell you that age has little to do with meat quality. Any critter moving *up* in physical conditioning — "on the mend," as they say — will make good meat. One that's declining won't. A ribby-looking whitetail seldom is good venison. Look for deer with rounded, smooth sides. If this rounding continues forward over the shoulders, chances are it's in top shape. Look also for rounded haunch contours, and for lack of any distinct drawn appearance just ahead of the hind legs.

"A buck with a gant flank," a Georgia hunter once told me, "isn't worth shooting unless he's wearing a tremendous set of horns."

Another key to condition that I always check is the neck. A buck coming into or in rut will usually have a swollen neck. If the neck of either sex looks extra-long and scrawny, the deer probably isn't much for meat. If vertebrae outlines show along the ridge of the back, or hip bones are apparent, the animal is guaranteed to be thin and tough.

But the best indicator of a whitetail's condition is its coat. These critters go through two color phases: they wear a reddish coat in summer and a gray one in winter. By October, the red should be completely gone, and you should pass up any animal that still shows red at this time. Look particularly for a glossy coat, and a thick one. A dull, patchy pelt is a sign that says, "Don't shoot."

Becoming a meat hunter doesn't mean you should quit hunting whitetails with trophy antlers. If you find those, shoot! Where the average whitetail is concerned, however, there are no trophy decisions to make; thus the meat becomes the important consideration. By keeping that in focus, you can enhance your whitetail hunt immeasurably — and enjoy the results every time you sit down to a venison meal.

Guide brings a good mule deer buck down from rugged daw where it was shot. For mule deer you can make a practice of hunting draws only in mountain country with high success.

Mule deer feeds on piñon nuts in the mouth of a wide draw.

CHAPTER 12

THE LUCK OF THE DRAW
FOR MULE DEER

Author took this good mule deer buck
in rugged, rocky draw where it had
bedded down.

During a mule deer hunt a good many years ago in eastern Montana, a guide took me up a snug, deep draw in which I promptly tagged a heavy-antlered buck the first day. As we sat resting after work was done, I remarked that he certainly seemed to know where to hunt. He smiled whimsically and said, "I learned when I started hunting for a living that if I stuck to the draws for muleys I could send hunters home happy and help pay my bills."

Often afterward, reminiscing about various mule deer hunts over many years and seven states, I've thought of that. Some years I hunted two or more states the same fall for several seasons, way back when two to as many as four bucks were legal. Of well over fifty muleys taken, remembering as accurately as possible the circumstances of each hunt, I'd guess I collected 60 to 70 percent of them while hunting the draws.

A portion of that success, obviously, was because I *hunted* draws. But the *reason* I hunted them was precisely the same as that of the Montana guide years before — high success.

After that opener I had to wait several days on companions who continued hunting. Thinking about what the guide had said, I spent the time watching deer. At first shooting light some might be down on flats bordering foothills, feeding, usually near a draw and ready to move into or along it on their way to bed down upslope, the usual muley direction.

By 8:30 to 9:30 on an average morning, you could glass deer along the edges of draws, or along inner faces of large ones. If there was water, perhaps a seep or live creek, or a cattle tank near a draw mouth, they'd pause to drink on their way up. Most days you didn't see them after the full warmth of the sun was bathing the ridges, unless you glassed the rims meticulously above the heads of the defiles, the inner faces of the draws, or walked up them to jump deer out. By 3:30 to 4:30 in the afternoon, once again I'd drive around or sit and glass and see deer coming out of the draws, feeding the edges, fiddling along after moving downward toward flats or even an alfalfa field.

A "draw" can mean several different types of terrain features, depending on where you are. One dictionary defines it as a "land basin into or through which water drains." That's a bit too general. The word "draw," when denoting a land feature, did originate with water — drawing off water by gravity flow. A sharp, snug canyon is a kind of draw. So is a dry wash, which runs or is wet only when there's rain. A live stream, gully, coulee, dry gulch, or eroded cleft in the earth are all varied types of draws. Every mountain has fold after fold vertically slanted into its sides — draws — some of bare rock edged by brush, some forested along their edges, some choked with brush, each type scribed to its dimensions by a particular gradient and expanse of watershed.

Indeed, water is the key. Because draws are tilted, water runs down all kinds, in the case of a live creek constantly, in numerous other types intermittently. Because of the water, vegetation of countless variety grows abundantly along them. Here is forage for mule deer, plus bedding places in brush, aspen, or juniper. At the mouths of many draws forage is especially lush. Somewhere along most draws there'll be shady areas on one side or the other at any time of day. A deer has but to move a few yards when the sun gets too warm in order to find cooler comfort.

In deep erosions snaking across rough foothills, there are overhangs, sometimes seeps. Tenacious clumps of tough vegetation form cool resting places. Further, draws of all types in mule deer domain are the most natural — and secluded and safest — travel routes. The draw has more of everything a mule deer needs in its bailiwick than any other feature of the landscape. It thus becomes a magnet.

I remember that Montana guide explaining as we visited all those years ago: "The hunting day during muley season is at best no more than 10 hours long. Of that 10, deer will be in or near the draws at least 6, often more. Sure, they'll be other places at times, and certain individual animals will be unpredictable mavericks in habits. The *bulk* of the herd, however, will conform. Why hunt helter-skelter when the luck of the draw is virtually assured?"

During several early hunts in Colorado and Wyoming, I became convinced mule deer country was far more complicated for a hunter to decipher than whitetail habitat. I recall looking at a massive sweep of mountains in western Colorado and wondering how I'd ever locate a deer. The terrain was an overwhelming maze of intricate details. Unlike whitetail habitat, in which areas where deer rest, feed, and travel are rather predictable and easily spotted, this was one enormous puzzle. A deer could be anywhere.

Riding horseback that day, alone, half lost most of the time, I did jump a deer here and there, without much seeming reason. They really did seem to be anywhere. But I recalled meanwhile a curious fact concerning the natural history of mule deer that led in round about fashion to success several hours later. Over their hundreds of years of existence, muleys never were able to successfully colonize flat country. Level woodlands, where whitetails thrive, or prairies were often barriers to range expansion.

The muleys established themselves over an enormous north-south region, from the 60th parallel in the far north deep into Mexico — always in and along mountains and foothills. From west to east, however, in the last broken eastern country separating foothills from interior plains, their colonization ended. Wherever these deer are found on the western fringe of the plains, there invariably are skeins of creeks, erosions, river-bottom breaks. For optimum habitat, mule deer need rugged, steep terrain, or at the least pronouncedly undulating foothills of broken brushlands.

A biologist friend who has long worked with mule deer says it best. "Muleys must have *sloped* country. In fact, every detail of their shape and muscular structure affirms it."

Looking at the puzzling Colorado vista, trying to sort it out to make sense, I thought about that and again of the Montana guide and his fixation on draws. Then it hit me: It is the slopes that *make* the draws. And what were the most distinctive and easily sorted out features of this mountain maze, as related to the daily lives of the deer I was after? It was suddenly simple. From where I sat in my saddle I could count four likely draws just by turning my head 90 degrees. I tied my horse, walked up, and took a high vantage point overlooking one of the draws, then put the big maze out of mind, and about 4 P.M. had my buck on the ground.

Any mule deer hunter in strange country can easily orient himself by following the draw method. Forget the deer that are "just anywhere" without seeming good reason. Look over an expanse of country, focus on the draws. Even if you are acquainted with an area, this method is a short cut. You wander less, spend less effort where deer *may* be, more where odds are better. Obviously, if you work a draw where there is no sign, you'd better leave it for another. This physical feature gives you instant focus and direction, even in totally strange country.

For several seasons early in my mule deer years I hunted an area in northeastern Wyoming, desolate, wide-open country, still barely inhabited, in the general region where Crazy Woman Creek comes up from the south, some 50 miles northwest of Gillette, crosses old U.S. 14-16, and meanders on eventually to join the Powder River. Looking at it casually, you wouldn't believe mule deer would or could live here. Rough, treeless grazing lands roll endlessly westward toward the distant Bighorns.

Where would a deer hide, or feed? Walking this land or traveling by 4WD or horse, you soon find out. Red shale hills heave up here and there. Among them and across the humped-up emptiness you discover occasional enormous gullies eroded into these roughs. Some snake for miles, 40 feet deep in places. They're the key. Walk the bottom of one and sometimes the walls almost touch overhead. At other places the gully is wide. Seeps are abundant. Brush patches cling to the contours.

I used to drive around there at night with a rancher friend, shooting jackrabbits. Deer were always skipping away out of the vehicle lights. They were all over the open country after dark. But what is so classic here is that come daylight most of them are back in the easily noted gullies. A few find refuge in scattered brush clumps, or on the shale hummocks. Look at the gully bottom, however, and you'll find deer tracks all around. Look over the entire vast sweep of country and you instantly know these draws are the only places of consequence for deer to retire to, the *only* places to concentrate your hunting.

The biggest muley I've taken came out of one of those erosions. I walked the top, a companion the bottom. Unlike whitetails, which when disturbed would usually run along the bottom, mule deer want to get up top. They plunge up the side, sometimes where it's so steep you think they can't make it. That's what this one did — and he came right to me.

This open country, incidentally, illustrates a type of muley range too often overlooked. Without the draws — which many hunters passing by don't realize are there — the deer couldn't be there either. Other kinds of draws have to be viewed differently, and often hunted quite differently, too.

With a companion one fall I was hunting the Dixie National Forest out of Panguitch, Utah, with a couple of astute locals. There'd been a mixup about horses. We had only two. Our hosts, intimately acquainted with the country, said they'd put us atop a certain mountain to do some sitting and they'd take their chances riding the lower country. I'm not much of a sitter. I elected to ride. The other two left in a pickup and the remaining native and I separated and started out.

It was one of the toughest horseback rides I've ever had, in and out of timber, over rocks, dipping into wide draws and up the other rugged sides. At one point, shortly after we'd started, I was where I could look far up to the top of the mountain. I glimpsed color, raised my glass, and spotted the other local hunter in his red shirt hunkered down patiently on stand. It seemed silly in this enormous expanse. Even with the tough going, I was glad I was moving.

An hour passed. I saw not a deer. Then I heard a shot far above. Half an hour later there was another. I returned to our prearranged meeting place about noon, having seen not a hair. They were there with the pickup, two beautiful bucks in the back.

"I hated to shoot," the successful red-shirt said apologetically. "I wanted you to have the chance. You see, those draws you were crossing are all wide where you were, at the bottom, but up top where they start, they're narrow. That's why I wanted you up there. Your horse was just moving deer out and up their habitual travel routes to the top. We watched the heads of two draws close together, passed up three smaller deer, and whacked these two."

The lesson was not lost on me. Several times a single companion and I have managed similar drives. A proper whitetail drive might require in level country half a dozen or more hunters. By selecting a V-shaped draw, two can easily trick mule deer. Almost without fail, mule deer when moved from a resting place will go up. A sharp, narrow canyon or gulch with steep sides is perfect. One hunter prowls up the bottom, the other is stationed above near the head, watching sides and bottom. On two fairly recent occasions in western Texas two of us have run this scheme and the prowler, moving slowly and quietly, has shot a buck and put another to the hunter on stand.

One shouldn't think only in terms of wide canyons or large draws. For example, in steep sagebrush foothills at lower elevations, look at the narrow defiles up toward the top and you'll often see where aspen has taken hold in the head of a fold of terrain. These pockets, or the aspen strip marching down the draw running from one, are invariably deer havens. Especially in more open lower-range muley country and desert mule deer range, a draw you can jump across, where forage and brush grows, may harbor an old loner. Any dry wash with scrub along its banks may serve as a travel route, with branches coming into it, for deer moving from one mountain to another across several miles of flat, open low country.

Nor do you always have to walk the draws to jump targets or move them out. I've cruised trails in a vehicle, pausing often to glass, or sat high on a slope where I could glass much of it near and far, looking across several defiles, and watched deer move out or in, or feed along the faces or crowns. Some may be close enough for a shot. Others can be stalked.

It's not so much how you elect to hunt the draws as it is getting fixed in your mind that they are the most important, distinctive physical features of a mule deer's domain, most attractive and useful to the animals, most easily identified by the hunter. It doesn't matter that some deer may be scattered elsewhere in other terrain. Those deer are a gamble, but the luck of the draw is always built in.

Mule deer appear on ridge, and startle hunter who is far from ready.

This photo shows how contriving a rest in an instant can be done. Hunter sneaking up draw drops beside a chunk of downed timber that will serve as rifle rest.

CHAPTER 13

BE READY WHEN THE DEER IS

Deer often force one into instant readiness. Here neck shot is presented, but hunter must be quick.

One fall while still-hunting for whitetail deer, I slowly worked out a strip of timber, gun at the ready every second. Coming to the end of the trees without sighting a target, I swung my rifle sling over my shoulder and started across an open, tall-grass field of possibly 50 acres. On the far side was another plot of likely timber.

Halfway across, I was startled to see a handsome eight-point buck rise from its bed in the grass, way out here in the open. It, too, was startled. It stood for perhaps 5 seconds, broadside, and stared. Then it ran like blazes. I simply stood and gawked. No buck was *supposed* to be bedded down out here in the open!

Every deer hunter, I'm sure, has been involved in comparable situations. The problem is invariably the same. The deer appears during one of those moments when the hunter isn't ready or is unable to do the shooting. Trying to think of all the situations that might thwart a shot isn't easy. Nonetheless, as most expert deer hunters agree, incessant high-key alertness and detailed plotting are essential to success.

A Wisconsin hunter whose den wall is covered with trophy-size heads explained this the best I've heard. "Many hunters," he told me, "fail to understand the imbalance between hunting time and shooting time. Think of it like this: During deer season there probably will be an average of 10 hours of hunting light each day. If you're fortunate enough to have a week to hunt, that's 70 hours. Maybe you'll get several opportunities for shots. Or perhaps you'll get only one, or at least only one at a deer you really want."

Most chances, he pointed out, come and go in no more than 10 seconds. So given 70 hours of hunting time, there may be only 10 seconds of shooting time buried somewhere in them. Even if several opportunities are presented, and they're longer than 10 seconds, at best you'll have only a couple of minutes out of 70 hours to make it a successful hunt.

"There's no way," he concluded, "to predict when any one of these brief periods may occur. A deer hunter who is successful most of the time has to be ready *all* of the time!"

That buck bedded in the open grass field taught me one of the specific lessons of alertness. General experience, and reams of deer hunting literature, teach that when deer, especially whitetails, are resting, they are always in dense cover. But "always" is a word that should be deleted from the deer hunter's dictionary. *Most* deer rest in heavy cover. However, an individual deer may be, at any time, anywhere it wants to be, which means that it may be . . . anywhere.

The hunter who stays cocked, always expecting the unexpected, is the one who has the advantage when an opportunity arises.

Much of the art of staying ready concerns alertness to small details. A classic example of failing to follow this advice took place during a mule deer hunt I made with a friend in western Texas. We were driving during midday on a large ranch, pausing to glass for deer. I was at the wheel, and my friend was to do the shooting. We finally spotted a big ten-point rack silhouetted against bright yellow grass. The deer was lying in shade beneath a piñon.

The small pine was the only tree in the area. A low, grass-covered ridge ran up to the right. Fifty yards upslope a motte of shinoak not much taller than a deer spread over an expanse of possibly 30 yards. My companion, hopping with excitement, got out, and, hurriedly circling left, began a sneak, hoping to get within close range.

Presently he appeared, bellying over a small hummock not more than 75 yards below the bedded trophy. It looked so easy, but a critical detail had been overlooked. Because the grass was tall, both he and the buck would have to get up for him to place a shot.

The buck rose. The hunter started to. The deer whirled and bolted up the ridge, behind the single piñon. The hunter by then was moving aside, trying to clear the pine, the branches of which now screened the deer from his view because of the angle of the slope. By the time my friend got into position, the buck had wheeled around the shinoak motte; and before he could move again, the deer was over the ridge.

Afterward he admitted he'd been impetuous, and we discussed how it should have been done. Had he looked the layout over carefully, then circled *right*, behind the low ridge, he could have come back over and downslope, covered by the shinoak patch. A sneak around its end, rifle ready, would have allowed him to shoot from above at close range, over the grass. The buck probably could have been killed in its bed.

Indeed, the lament, "There was just that one tree in the way!" has for years been a minor-key dirge sung by hunters in practically every deer camp in the nation. Few who sing it seem to realize that *they* put the tree in the way by poor planning. Whether you're on a stand or still-hunting, meticulous attention to trees and land contours that could become shot spoilers will help keep you watching, or moving, so you'll be ready when a deer is.

There are numerous other situations of which to be cognizant, and to avoid or use to your advantage. Light direction is one. When my

sons, Mike and Terry, were beginning to hunt deer, one of my instructions was a basic rule I've long followed. On bright days, hunt west
early in the morning, and east late in the day, unless the breeze direction makes it impossible, in which case, hunt north or south.

I pointed out that there are two reasons for this. When you face
bright light from a low-slanted sun, in numerous instances your scope
becomes useless, overwhelmed by brightness. Also, if breeze direction, or lack of one, allows you to put the sun directly at your back,
you have deer at a disadvantage. Staring into bright sun inhibits their
vision just as badly as it does yours.

Mike and Terry were youngsters then, and during that period they
didn't think the Old Man was nearly as smart as he later became. They
didn't pay much attention, so it amused me when each in turn came
to me full of frustration with a tale about a buck that stood and stared
as they desperately tried to see him through a scope, looking into the
sun. The Old Man's wisdom suddenly was amazing.

Oddly, a surprising number of unready moments occur where
they'd be least expected, and most easily avoided, to hunters on stands.
Three that I can think of offhand are typical.

"I had built myself a seat in a tree," one sad story goes. "There
was one limb I straddled. I had my gun on the right side of it when
a deer appeared to the left. When I moved my gun I clunked the limb,
and the buck was gone. It was plain dumb not to have cut it off in the
first place."

"I was sitting on stand, gun ready, with a good rest," runs the
second lament. "A real trophy buck appeared, close. I moved my foot
and there was this stick that popped. You can bet I've cleaned every
twig from stands I've used since."

The third tale of woe goes like this: "A wet year had resulted in
tall grass covering openings. I was sitting down, and not until the deer
showed did it dawn on me that the grass was as tall as the deer. I'd
have to shoot through many yards of the stuff, and I did. Maybe not
every bullet would have been deflected, but mine was. It was a valuable
lesson."

It's difficult for a hunter to anticipate all the problems that may
crop up. Some you simply have to experience. The best example of
this happened to an archer friend with whom I was hunting mule deer
in open country. We'd built a small blind of sagebrush on a hillside
above a creek waterhole, near which was a welter of deer tracks. Short
sage grew around the pond.

The plan was to wait for a suitable buck to come in to drink. When it put its head down to the water, the short sage would be above its eyes. The archer would slowly rise and shoot down on it over the front of the blind.

The first two deer to come in were does. My friend decided to make a practice draw on them. As they started to drink, he made his play. The deer flushed in a panic. We had no idea why. The next deer was a most desirable buck. When its head was lowered, the archer again eased up. The same thing happened. Before he could get off an arrow, the buck all but turned wrong side out getting away.

Not until I went down to the waterhole and had him rise and draw his bow did we dope out what was wrong. His movement and figure were perfectly mirrored in the water. To the drinking deer, he appeared to be rising right at them out of the pool.

Much of deer hunting lore is concerned with thwarting the animals' three keen senses. Most hunters understand this and follow the obvious rules. They hunt across a breeze to keep deer from scenting them. They use various ruses to keep deer from seeing them, and realize that motion, not necessarily the shape of an immobile human form, is what draws the attention of the quarry and often frightens it. Yet there are always those errors, like the image in the pool, that result in the deer being readier than you are.

Among these are *small* sounds. Deer hearing is acute. Animals that haven't yet seen or scented danger are often especially uneasy about noises they don't understand, particularly ones repeated at rhythmic intervals. I hunted one fall with a fellow who wore a squeaky boot. The day was still and damp, and every step he took — *squeak squeak*. I moved off to hunt on my own, and I could still hear him many yards distant. I saw several deer and shot a doe. When we got back together he told me he'd seen nothing.

I recall another still-hunter who carried a rifle with a sling swivel that tinkled and rattled. He was so used to it that I doubt he even heard it. Deer may not be afraid of such unnatural sounds, but you can bet those sounds will direct their attention toward you, which is the last thing you want.

What causes the most ruined opportunities? For several seasons I asked this question of hunters I met, and urged them to tell me their sad tales. The consensus (by a wide margin) was that the majority of foulups were due to lack of a rest, or a poorly chosen one.

A still-hunter friend missed what he claimed was the top trophy of all his hunting years because he tried an off-hand shot. A few hunters, to be sure, are good at shooting offhand. This is not, however, a very sensible or accurate way to shoot a rifle. Most hunters miss more than they hit when trying it, or wound deer.

This hunter now operates as if he's hunting rests as diligently as deer. "I'm constantly aware of vertical saplings, stumps, blowdowns, large boulders, fenceposts — anything that will serve for a solid rest. I still-hunt so I'm always near a quick rifle rest."

Setting up a proper rest on a stand is just as important. Where can a deer appear? What will serve most quickly and efficiently to cover all the possibilities? Some rests may place your barrel too high or too low; others may allow you to steady your rifle only at a certain angle.

The most ingenious rest arrangement I've seen was shown me by a rancher friend in Texas. He sat me beside a small post oak on a low rock bluff overlooking a narrow, wooded valley. He picked up a stout stick about 5 feet long, jabbed one end into the ground at my left and leaned the other into a crotch of the oak on my right side near my head. The stick thus slanted from right to left in front of me.

"If a deer appears far down the valley, grab the stick high up with your left hand and lay the fore-end across the stick and your fist. For any shooting angle that's closer, even to right below you, just slide your hand down the stick and let the rifle follow. You can also move the barrel left or right at any height, to cover the width of the valley."

This rest worked beautifully. In fact, when a buck appeared close below, I slid my hand down, the rifle barrel following. The crosshair settled steadily, and I put the deer down. I've used this rest numerous times since when on a stand. It's always a reminder that no amount of deer hunting lore you may have stored up makes much difference unless you train yourself to be ready . . . always.

Hunters resting in camp during midday waste good hunting time.

Deer routinely move from a midday bed, wander a bit, then lie down again.

CHAPTER 14
THE MIDDAY DEER HUNTER

Author takes his own advice. Hunting during middle of the day, this whitetail was spotted picking up acorns among scrub oaks.

Ever since deer have been hunted, hunters have been concentrating on the early morning and late afternoon hours. The smart hunter, so deer-hunt lore goes, may as well spend the middle of the day in camp because the deer aren't moving. Maybe it's time for these hunters to become full-time instead of part-time operatives and consider hunting in the middle of the day. Maybe most hunters don't really know what deer are doing during the bulk of the day because they aren't in the woods trying to find out.

When I was a young deer hunter I stayed with it all day, mostly because I was ridiculously eager, but also because I've never been a midday napper. Older deer hunters, who were my mentors during my first seasons, tried to explain to me that I was wasting good camp-resting time, but I kept at it, regardless. Happily, an early experience so firmly convinced me of the validity of midday hunting that I've been an all-day deer hunter much of the time since — and have turned a surprising number of deer into venison during those supposedly non-productive hunting hours.

That first midday deer was admittedly plain luck, but it made a lasting impression. I was living in northern Michigan and had been invited to hunt with a group who were staying in a cabin on a half-section of privately owned land in the middle of a large state forest. I was unable to get out there the night before opening day, and was exasperatingly held up the next morning. I finally arrived at the locked gate about 11:30 A.M., parked my car in the woods, and got ready to walk the mile and a half to the cabin. Someone would bring me out later to pick up my vehicle.

Naturally I was alert for deer as I walked slowly, pausing intermittently, along the old woods trail. The day was utterly still, overcast, not a wisp of air stirring. When I was within a quarter-mile of the cabin, I looked at my watch. High noon. On my right was a low ridge cut by a small saddle with cover of balsams, poplar, and birch. On my left and possibly 50 yards distant was a trout stream running parallel to the road and ridge. I paused, listening to the subdued music of the river.

Suddenly I heard something — *splash, splash, splash*. A deer, crossing the river? I stepped off the road toward the saddle and in among a scattering of balsams, excitement all but overwhelming me, glimpsed a brief flicker of tawny-gray. Then I actually heard the deer as it reached the trail and trotted along it, surely coming my way. The saddle! A natural crossing point.

The first part of the animal I saw was its head — with antlers. Not very large. But I wasn't a very large deer hunter at that time, either. The deer turned off the road, paused to nibble a leaf, took several steps, and was broadside to me, wide open, unaware, and not an inch over 5 yards away. I had my rifle up, but I was so close and excited I darned near missed the animal. A half-inch higher and the bullet would have done nothing but make the hair fly.

This one chance meeting obviously could be construed to prove much, or nothing, depending on who was doing the construing. Make no mistake — I have no intention of low-rating early and late hunting. Like most other deer hunters, and writers about deer hunting, I've repeated countless times that hunters have their best chances when deer are actively moving about and feeding, thus exposing themselves, and that without question the two basic foraging periods are early morning and later afternoon.

The fact remains, however, that few hunters know anything at all about how deer spend the middle of their day. Sure, they lie down. Deer are cud chewers, like cattle. They fill their bellies, then find a pleasant, comfortable, hopefully safe resting place, and finish the digestive process via cud chewing. But do they spend the whole day at it? Let's presume that a deer is on range where forage is abundant. Let's suppose it can fill up in an hour with ease. It is ready to bed down as early as 8 A.M. Does it lie there dreaming until 4 P.M. — for eight solid hours?

I've seen mule deer on several occasions get out of beds under a rimrock running generally north-south and move up and over as the sun moved. They had selected lie-up spots that were shady and cool in the morning, on the west slope. When the sun reached that side they moved back to the east slope.

During severe weather, and especially where snow is deep, bear in mind that deer require more food than they do in a mild climate. They quite commonly forage during the middle of the day to take up the slack.

When a deer has bedded down after its morning feeding period, regardless of the time, and lies for an hour or more, it is virtually certain to change positions. Deer observed in captivity prove the contention. The deer may hitch around some and finally get to its feet, then move a few steps, stretching muscles. It urinates, empties its bowels. A close observation of bedding places where deer have matted down grass invariably shows a considerable amount of droppings nearby. And rather often there will be other beds nearby indicating that the deer wandered off and then lay down again.

A most enlightening study of deer movements ws done at the Welder Wildlife Foundation in Texas. The results are an eye-opener for hunters who are sitting out midday in camp. The research, done by Texas A&M University with a team under the direction of Professor Jack M. Inglis, lasted for a year. The deer were fitted with tiny radio transmitters and kept track of by central sensing equipment.

In correspondence, Inglis told me, "It was possible for us to detect when deer were up and around by interpreting radio signals. Such activity doesn't imply that the deer were moving cross country, but only that they were on their feet and active."

One of the researchers, he added, in some instances actually approached the animals to visually verify what was going on.

The study, he assured, thoroughly corroborated the beliefs and practices of early and late deer hunters. There was indeed an emphatic increase in activity shortly before dawn. Deer moved to feeding areas and fed, dependent upon weather and amount of human disturbance, for anywhere from one to four hours. There are clues here for astute hunters. When the woods are crowded with hunters, this early-morning activity period is certain to be interrupted. Certainly many deer are killed because one hunter spooks them into the line of sight of another. But a crowded forest has its disadvantages, too. It influences deer to get into hiding cover as quickly as possible, and often to feed in places they might not normally select.

Further, the abundance or scarcity of forage is directly related to the length of the morning activity. A food scarcity that forces deer to search longer in order to fill their stomachs obviously lengthens the activity period in the morning.

However, under normal conditions, hunters leave their stands by midmorning because the deer have moved into resting cover. Make note that hunter disturbance lessens at that same time. Don't think for a moment the deer aren't aware of this. At noon and often from as early as 10:30 A.M. until at least 2:30 P.M. the deer feel more confident, for the hunters are out of the woods. A deer that has been disturbed at breakfast may well move out at least along the edges of its hiding and loafing areas to grab a few more bites. Conversely, if the deer has filled up quickly in the early morning and gone to its bedding ground early, it is getting uneasy and restless by noon.

The A&M study, which authenticated this, showed that after a late or midmorning period of inactivity, midday activity rose to a peak. As Professor Inglis cautioned, this didn't mean the deer were roving all about. What they were doing was looking for shadier places to rebed, or they sporadically browsed, moved along edges of the resting cover, or lazed around in it on their feet. Because I have long been an all-day hunter whenever possible, I have watched deer time after time making these movements during midday.

There is, in fact, a dense cedar brake on our ranch where I suppose over the past twenty years thirty or forty deer of all sizes and both sexes have been bagged. The cedars are tall and spreading, fairly open underneath. There is total shade; the area is high and gets a good breeze, uninhibited by dense undergrowth. This brake is not easy to see into, yet is open enough near ground level for deer to see out, and a sharp-eyed hunter to spot deer in. We regularly hunt along its edge during the middle of every day. Often deer are seen lying down, and just as often standing or moving around.

The midday activity period, as the A&M study indicated, is mostly within cover in typical bedding or resting areas, and along their edges. The study further shows that the high-activity period during midday is followed, on days of average normal weather conditions, by a period of inactivity during the early half of the afternoon. As most hunters know, the early afternoon lull is followed by the major late afternoon foraging period. This may begin very late, depending on weather, food, and hunter disturbance. Under perfect hunting conditions, it starts around 3 or 4 P.M., but may not occur until dusk, and if disturbance is severe, the deer may wait until after dark to begin moving and feeding. It's that period from late morning through early afternoon that deer hunters accustomed to sitting it out should consider.

There is one more useful, even surprising bit of lore uncovered by the study. Many of us have watched deer go to water at 8 or 9 in the morning on their way to bedding grounds. Of course, deer can and do drink almost anywhere, so distinct water treks aren't always noticeable. In the arid portions of the state where I live, we sometimes are able to witness the drinking routine because places to drink are limited, especially during dry times. The radio-fitted deer, it was discovered, quite often made a trip to water at the end of the midday peak of activity and prior to bedding down again in time for the early afternoon lull.

Hunters should not misconstrue this information. You aren't going to see a whole herd of deer streaming out of a thicket and heading for the creek for a drink at 1 P.M. But *one* buck may wander out of its safe haven to get a drink, and if you know this may happen — and you aren't snoring in camp — he may wear your tag.

Hunters should not get the idea they are going to quit the midday camp-sitting, get back into the woods, and see deer cavorting behind every bush. Deer, like all creatures, are individuals. One may feed heartily through the middle of the day, roaming around. Another may only turn in its bed and go back to dozing. But midday activity does occur, and under optimum conditions there is a pronounced flurry of it.

The usual method pursued by the all-day deer hunter is to get into cover during the middle of the day and prowl slowly, trying to catch a deer in its bed. Only very few hunters become adept at this kind of hunting. Most move too fast and too noisily, and succeed only in putting deer out unseen ahead of them. The expert still-hunter certainly doesn't need to change his tactics. But adding the knowledge of interim deer activity may give him an edge. For the bumbling prowler, this is a perfect time to pick a spot *in* cover, and simply sit.

The main point to be made is that every hunter gets only so many days each year to hunt. A great many get only a single trip of two or three days' duration. Why waste half your hunting time in camp? Why not shave your odds on success by adding to your hunting hours? Granted, the majority of deer hunters are early and late operatives because they are convinced those are the best times, and no doubt they are right. But you'll never know how close midday can come to being good if you're sitting around camp telling tall tales.

Especially during the rut, a big stranger may show up that you've not previously known in the area.

Some excellent trophies are among the old traveling bucks.

CHAPTER 15
THOSE TRAVELING OLDSTER BUCKS

A buck like this one may suddenly appear in your hunting area where you've seen only modest racks.

Where I live in Texas, whitetail deer are extremely abundant, but small. Field-dressed 70-pounders are average, and a 100-pound buck is one to brag about. Yet every season a few comparative monsters turn up. As a rule, nobody has any idea where they came from. Usually they're taken purely by chance.

During my first year in Texas, I'd been invited to a small ranch where the owners knew every deer on their place. One evening a guest hunter from Houston was late coming in. They asked if I'd try to locate him.

I found him wild-eyed with excitement and exhausted, trying to drag a deer to his vehicle. When I got a close look, I was as excited as he. It was a stunning ten-pointer, heavy-antlered, and for this area an authentic monster. Field-dressed, the deer weighed 145 pounds.

I've always remembered what the rancher said as we weighed it: "That buck wasn't from around here. He's an itinerant."

Thinking about that, I recalled the numerous instances when someone — including me, occasionally — had bagged a trophy buck that was a "stranger." Few of the hunters who had lucked into such an animal had been purposely hunting it. However, I believe that a scattering of these eye-poppers are present anywhere you hunt, and so it's worth making a point now and then of planning a hunt for one.

The odds on such a hunt will be long, but occasionally it works. Itinerant bucks *are* real. They're usually older deer that have moved (chiefly during the rut) miles outside their home territories. On every hunting ground there are a few resident bucks that are old, long-settled, and awesomely wise. They move mostly at night and are masters at keeping their private lives private. Itinerants won't know the territory that well, and so may be more susceptible.

Itinerants and recluses are invariably five to eight years old. The three I've taken were seven, determined by standard jaw and tooth examination used by biologists. Studies in several states indicate that deer in this age group make up no more than 2 percent of the herd. Hunting them purposely, therefore, is a highly uncertain game, but a real challenge, and a great satisfaction when you happen to win.

A Michigan friend who has collected several reclusive old deer says, "Don't just hope you'll bumble into one while not really believing there are any where you hunt. Have faith that one or two *are* there. Then figure out where they're most likely to be. *Assume* them."

He points out that the Missouri monster given number one place in the Boone and Crockett non-typical records was an overlooked oldster. In 1982 it was found dead in a region where scores of hunters had operated. He adds that the buck that will probably replace it, a non-typical Ohio deer from a populous area, also was found dead. He is sure many more such super-wise old monsters are never discovered and die of old age.

Collecting an itinerant is mostly a matter of staying constantly alert for one, and concentrating your efforts at correct times and places. These bucks are *travelers*. A Texas study involving radio-collared mature bucks lost one big fellow from what was considered his home territory. He was located later, 6 miles away. He moved widely in that new area during the entire rut period, then he returned home.

A Texas friend who dotes on watching for traveling trophies points out that almost every one is spotted at first, or last, shooting light. "They don't give you much chance. They're always extremely nervous, partly because they're wise oldsters, but also because they're in strange territory and realize they aren't familiar with it."

He spends long hours watching or following groups of does, or mature singles, very early and very late. "The itinerants make a point of seeking them and looking them over, hoping to find a doe that hasn't been bred. The rut lasts, on a much reduced scale, far longer than most hunters are aware. Late in the season, keep watch for traveling bucks to show up where does are. Those bucks are especially vigorous, bullish, persistent, and bent on pursuing females in another buck's territory."

My experience has been that you should never overlook even the least likely location for one of these travelers to appear. For example, on our home place — 27 acres of oak and cedar surrounded by subdivisions — we feed resident deer in our yard but don't hunt them. Each year we come to recognize every animal.

Almost every season, a big stranger suddenly shows up, invariably at dawn or near dusk. He's always jumpy and seldom eats more than a nibble, if anything. But every one I've observed pesters and examines each doe. Then it leaves and we never see it again. These sudden, brief, nervous appearances illustrate how a hunter who hopes to bag an itinerant buck must first believe they exist, and then be ready at all times for instant action, no matter how unlikely the surroundings.

The hunter must also cultivate a sixth sense about where a big deer might show up. He must also be ready to play hunches. A striking example of this involved the largest whitetail I took during the years I lived in northern Michigan.

Just outside our small village was an old, abandoned house with open fields around it and a run-out apple orchard behind it. The rut was on. Snow covered the ground. Driving in from a state forest where

I'd been hunting, I noted at dusk a covey of does scrounging frozen apples in the old orchard.

To any standard-plan deer hunter, this was no place to find a big buck. A silly spike, maybe, but no oldster. There wasn't a speck of cover in any direction for 300 yards to the nearest timber. But suddenly I wondered. What about a *traveler*? I asked around, casually, if anybody had seen a big buck in that general area during the fall. No one had. Too open and too close to town, they all said.

I checked the orchard the next day and found it stippled with deer tracks, none large. But here, each day, was a dusk gathering of numerous does. Maybe, my hunch told me, a traveler would find this concentration and check it out. I sat in the old house, gun rested across a paneless window sill, and froze my tail for three evenings. That was enough. I quit, and went back to the forest the next afternoon. But I couldn't resist one more stakeout at the old house.

The doe contingent straggled in as the light was going; the clean snow held barely enough to outline a deer sharply. Suddenly, there he was, spooky but still bold as brass, stalking through the band of does. He cut one out. She ran. As he started his first bound to follow, I let him down.

In a small town, news moves fast. That heavy-antlered ten-pointer drew numerous lookers. Most interesting, three different people who lived over a couple of square miles surrounding that old orchard and knew every deer on their lands swore they'd briefly seen the traveler on the move at dawn or dusk over the past couple of days, but had never seen him previously. No doubt that this was an itinerant stranger.

Hunting resident recluses is in some ways similar, and in others, quite different. Like the travelers, the old settlers are almost wholly nocturnal. First and last shooting light are the only chances you get. The old bucks are never bold, but are sly schemers who select the least-suspected daytime hideouts. If you begin by assuming one lives in your hunting territory, then systematically list the most secluded hideouts, every now and then you'll nail one down. You don't wait for these deer to appear early or late on feeding grounds; you patiently watch a potential lair.

Once you've become convinced that an oldster dwells in a given area, you tick off possible hideouts. Be imaginative. Some may be obvious, but others may be where you simply wouldn't believe a deer could or would attempt to hide.

The all-time classic illustration of this, which might be used as a pattern by recluse hunters, was told to me by a North Dakota farmer with whom I once hunted. His land was flat, mostly tilled. There were two woodlots, each with understory cleared so they were too open to serve as more than temporary hideouts and travel routes for deer. For several years the farmer had been noticing an extra-large deer track. Often in the morning it would show near his barn, where he fed cattle. Although he annually killed a so-so buck along the willow-grown creeks meandering across his fields, he never saw the big one he suspected must live there. Finally, one fall morning, he was at the barn before full light and glimpsed a monster buck trotting toward one of the woodlots.

"I was excited," he told me, "but irked. How could that sly devil live right under my nose year after year and not show up *sometime* during daylight and in deer season?"

Out in the middle of a large hayfield, there were several small swales grown to dense, low willows and tough, tall weeds and grasses, around which he always mowed. Each was only about 50 yards in diameter, and the surrounding fields were completely open stubble.

"I never gave a thought to those when deer hunting. They were too small and isolated for a deer to dare use them. I'd never even checked for tracks around them."

Then one morning, following a fresh snow during deer season, he was driving across the farm to town when he happened to notice a track heading toward one of those little swales. He stopped and examined it. Big. Deep. Feet dragging. Keeping at a substantial distance, he drove clear around the swale. No track came out!

"I forgot town errands and farm work. I considered jumping him out. But he'd bolt out the opposite side and I'd never see him. Late that afternoon I went down the back side of the nearest woodlot, crossed it to where I could watch the swale. The range was about 250 yards. I settled down, got a steady rest, and waited — not very patiently. Without the snow I could never have seen him when, at almost full dusk, he stealthily stepped to the edge and looked the field over, his magnificent rack showing. At last he moved out, giving me a full broadside. That old monster weighed almost 300 pounds, gutted. Later I examined the swale. Signs showed plainly that he'd been lying up there daytimes, probably all year."

It's obvious from these incidents that purposely hunting itinerant and reclusive whitetails is no surefire tag-filler. It's for guessers and gamblers, for hunters who shrug off a good many no-deer seasons in order to play a hunch that finally and miraculously pays off — *big.*

Few eastern hunters realize the West offers excellent whitetail hunting. In some areas they are over-abundant.

Author checks abundant tracks along trickle of water in western mountains. In fairly open whitetail range in West, brushy creek bottoms or gullies will hold resident whitetails.

CHAPTER 16

HUNTING WESTERN WHITETAILS

Whitetails in the West require determined hunting. They usually are in ample cover, and often in rugged terrain.

If you were sitting in on a pow-wow in a deer camp and someone came up with the statement that for the best chance at a trophy whitetail you should hunt the West — either in the United States or southern Canada — you'd probably make a mental note not to listen to him any longer. But you should listen. It's true.

Practically all deer hunters think of the eastern half of this continent's deer range as whitetail country and the western half as mule deer domain. In a general way that's correct, simply because there aren't any mule deer in the eastern half. But by envisioning the West as practically solid mule deer country, a very substantial amount of top-quality whitetail hunting is too often overlooked. Many of the hunters who live in the West don't even realize it's there. The mule deer certainly does predominate in the West and where pockets of whitetails occur they are much more difficult to hunt. Their habits are secretive, and they stick to such dense cover that few native hunters go after them. Most visitors have a pre-fix on mule deer.

Draw a line from north to south, beginning in southeastern Manitoba on down the eastern border of the Dakotas and wind up along eastern Texas. That divides the continent's deer range just about in half. Now if you want a jolt, get out the record book and study it a bit. A check of the revised printing of the Boone and Crockett lists will show you something you may not be prepared to believe, the rather astonishing fact that a whopping *two-thirds* of all whitetail records since they've been kept have come from *west* of that line!

In one way that figure may be a little unfair, because it is based on the total number of record whitetail heads from the United States, southern Canada and northern Mexico. That total of course takes in the Coues, or Arizona whitetail, which is in a record class by itself because of its smaller size both of body and antlers. So all right, deduct all Coues deer records, and you *still* come up with the startling statistic that approximately *three-fifths* of all records for the large whitetails are from the western half.

You don't necessarily have to be interested in a record-book head for such figures to be important to you. It is well known that areas which produce an outstanding number of records also produce large numbers of deer that are real trophies whether or not they make the book. Further, deer of blood lines and from soil/vegetation combinations of habitat that produce numerous outstanding racks invariably turn out big-bodied deer also. In some instances the deer population in the area may not be overwhelming, but most of the individuals are really big fellows. Thus without question the West offers some of the best and best-quality whitetail hunting on the continent.

Which states and provinces the majority of these records have come out of are also eye-openers. Possibly the biggest surprise — you could win a bet on it any day — is that (again leaving out the little Coues deer) the largest number of both typical and nontypical record heads have come from Saskatchewan. Consider that figure against few for the great whitetail states of Maine, New York, Michigan, and Pennsylvania.

Other western highs show Texas slightly in the lead after Saskatchewan. Nebraska holds third place. Then comes Manitoba, followed by Montana of all places, then the Dakotas. Intriguingly, Washington State, which most hunters don't credit with any whitetails, is next. That's a hot clue for trophy hunters. Compare it, for example, to an eastern-half state like Wisconsin, always a high-score location. Wisconsin shows slightly more than 2½ times Washington — but Wisconsin has a whitetail herd averaging from ten to 14 times as large as Washington!

With the exception of Texas, which has the largest whitetail herd in the nation (estimated at 3½ million) and the highest kill (average 350,000), there are of course far more whitetailed deer east of our line than west of it. Some western states have none. In most of those that have whitetails the range is quite restricted. In addition, whitetail herds, compared to mule deer, are small. But in numerous locations the deer are busters, and the top rank showing they've made over many years in the record book well illustrates that there are a high percentage of excellent heads compared to the modest numbers of deer.

It is understandable that Eastern hunters are eager to try for mule deer simply for the different experience, and they aren't thinking of whitetails when they travel to the West. But it is possible in states where more than one deer may be taken to collect a whitetail also. There have been seasons (and may be again) in a few locations where taking a whitetail as a second deer was mandatory. In some of these areas whitetails are inclined to overpopulate because of lack of hunter attention. In addition, whitetails are more stubborn and successful colonizers than are mule deer and here and there they usurp mule deer range. Biologists in west Texas, for example, worry about the whitetail taking over in certain areas where ranges of the two species meet and overlap.

Although almost everyone agrees that the whitetail is far more difficult to hunt than the mule deer, hunter success is nonetheless high in some of the best western whitetail ranges. And in some of these spots, such as northeastern Wyoming, the deer are exceedingly abundant. Most have both whitetails and mule deer in the same general regions. But the types of terrain they each cling to differ, the whitetails always sticking to the heavier cover, such as along stream courses or in heavy brush and timber.

Before you start hunting, use as background knowledge the fact that there are — or were — 17 different types of whitetails within U.S., Canadian and northern Mexican borders. The so-called "type" species was the Virginia whitetail. Odd as it may seem, this big deer, the first seen by the Colonists on the eastern seaboard and therefore the one from which all others were named as subspecies, is today practically extinct. It came close to extinction years ago and has been so diluted with introduced blood that it probably no longer exists as a true type.

The same situation holds true in the West with the burly Kansas whitetail, another big subspecies now phased out by dilution. The Texas whitetail, another subspecies, is at its regal best in southern Texas, but it has several forms, large and small and intergrades, on the fringes of its range. The Dakota whitetail is the big, rugged deer of the stream valleys, the northern plains and the badlands of most of the Prairie Province ranges of Canada and on down into parts of the Dakotas, Nebraska, northeastern Colorado, and even portions of Montana and Wyoming. I've seen them in Dakota cornfields while pheasant hunting, so fat they can barely waddle.

The Northwest whitetail of southeastern British Columbia, western Alberta, parts of eastern Washington, northern Idaho, western Montana and Wyoming is in its prime range one of the best trophies of all. So that's the wide-angle picture. Following is a close-focus look at where the western whitetails are and where the hunting is best.

Although British Columbia hasn't shown up heavily in the record book, you can find excellent hunting for a modest population of large whitetails here. There are three chiefs locations. Easiest to get into is the Kootenay River region of the extreme southeast. A second good bet is in the Okanagan valley of south-central British Columbia. And a third is the Peace River area of the eastern border. Most of the southeast has a fair whitetail population.

In Alberta, while the mule deer has drastically declined over the past years, whitetails have spread their range. Although the range is now across most of southern Alberta, heaviest population is based on the parklands of the east. Hunting rates as excellent.

It is even better to the east, in neighboring Saskatchewan. Here the whitetail is the most important big-game species. Although there are some mule deer, whitetails overwhelmingly predominate, making up an average 90 percent of the total deer kill. There are whitetails all throughout the southern half of the province, but harvest figures show that by far the hottest location, and one where success runs high, is in the southeast. This is all country with numerous roads and easily accessible. Chances of collecting a trophy head are good.

In Manitoba the whitetail is also the most important big-game variety. Curiously, during early settlement days here deer were almost nil. Lumbering and agriculture soon formed proper habitat, and the whitetails moved in. They now range far into the north, but the dense population spots are as follows: the southeast; the southwest farm country; the Interlake Region, which means the area between Lake Manitoba and Lake Winnipeg.

In Washington, as in British Columbia and eastward into part of Idaho and Montana, the big Northwest subspecies ranges. A characteristic of this deer is not only large body size but very widespreading antlers. Three counties in Washington turn out the preponderance of the kill: Stevens, Pend Oreille and the northern part of Spokane counties.

The Kanisku National Forest is located here, and much of the hunting is based on it and its fringes and along the stream courses of the region. It is estimated that not more than 10 percent of the total Washington deer herd are whitetails. But they are all packed into the extreme northeast. There are a very few Columbian whitetails in the southwest corner of the state.

Oregon has a remnant whitetail population in Wallowa County in the far northeast. There are also a few Columbian whitetails along the Columbia River in the northwest, and a scattering farther south.

Idaho has some sporty whitetail hunting, because the cover is dense. Virtually all whitetails in the state range north of the Salmon River, where a substantial number of residents hunt them. Of an average annual harvest in Idaho about 15 percent are whitetails. The deer are abundant over much of the northern Panhandle, where there are several National Forests. The fringes of these forests, and cover in settled areas of the Panhandle, offer the prime hunting opportunities.

Montana has a large whitetail population. In fact, there have been seasons when more than 25,000 whitetails were bagged. On the average they make up roughly a quarter of the total deer harvest. In some hunt units only whitetails are legal during most seasons. Two subspecies are found in the state, both of them large deer, the Northwest whitetail and the Dakota whitetail.

Some of the best hunting is in the northwest, most of it in Flathead, Lincoln, Sanders, Powell and Mineral counties. But the hunting is not easy. The cover is dense in the National Forests and along stream bottoms. Across the Divide, to the east, whitetails stick almost entirely to stream-course terrain. They range rather widely from the region along the Little Missouri in the southeast and on into the northern part of the state. But two locations offer highest populations. These are the Snowy Mountains out of Lewiston and portions of the Lewis and Clark National Forest. Whitetails are far more abundant than mule deer in those places.

Practically all the whitetails bagged in Wyoming come out of Crook County, in the northeastern corner of the state. This is the Black Hills area, where the Black Hills National Forest is located. There are also mule deer in this region. In some seasons in the past much of the total state deer kill has originated in what is known as the Black Hills Management Area. That well illustrates a heavy deer population. Often the kill is split about evenly between the two species.

Colorado is by no means a high-rating state for whitetails, but there are some. Most are fairly new immigrants. They began showing up in the northeast some years ago, apparently moving in from Kansas to the stream courses where habitat was most suitable. There was also a transplant of Oklahoma whitetails into the region at one time. Country along the South Platte and the Republican Rivers contains the largest populations.

In the extreme southwestern mountain ranges of New Mexico, and across in the southeastern quarter of Arizona, there is the range of the handsome but diminutive Coues deer, sometimes called fantail or Arizona whitetail. This is the only whitetail in Arizona, although New Mexico has a scattering of Texas whitetails east of Raton and also in the Lincoln National Forest. The little Coues is a true trophy with heavy, basket-like rack. Bucks seldom weigh over 100 pounds and many are smaller.

In New Mexico the largest population ranges Hidalgo County in the Peloncillo and Animas mountains. A lot of this country is virtually roadless, except for 4WD trails. There are also a few pockets worth trying a bit farther north, in the Gila National Forest. Across in Arizona the Coues range is larger. The oak, juniper and grass zone at around

6000 feet in the individual mountain ranges is usually best. Some good ranges: The Catalinas, Santa Ritas, Huachucas, Santa Teresa, Grahams, Galiuros, Chiricahuas, Tumacacoris. Numerous local guides make a specialty of hunting this deer.

Whitetails range over all of North Dakota and are by far the predominant species. But because of land-use changes and the building some years ago of the huge impoundments on the Missouri River, there have been numerous and continuing shifts of population. Fortunately, the state has a great many public hunting areas, and deer hunting is good in most of them. There are also the National Grasslands in the west. If any locations can be tagged as "best" it would be wooded stream courses almost anywhere in the state.

South Dakota also has whitetails statewide, and here also they far outnumber mule deer. Although there are a substantial number of deer in the farm region east of the Missouri, usually this is restricted to resident hunting. West of the Missouri, in what is called the West River Prairie, there is top-quality hunting usually with extremely high success. There are mule deer here also, but whitetails are most numerous. In the forested Black Hills region whitetails predominate and are abundant. Success is somewhat lower than in the more open terrain of the West Prairie.

Nebraska is one of the truly remarkable whitetail states because of the high number of record and trophy animals. Whitetails predominate in the east, mule deer in the west, but there is much overlapping. Ordinarily more mule deer than whitetails are killed, but success is very high on both. In general the southeastern counties, the northeastern Missouri River region and the central portion of the Niobrara River show the most whitetails taken and the highest success on them.

Generally, deer hunting in Kansas has been for residents only. For many years deer here were all but extinct, but a good herd has been building. Some very large whitetails are taken every season, most along stream courses of the east and north-central regions. Although Oklahoma does not have an enormous deer herd, the state does have some areas of amazingly high population density, and many bragging-size bucks bagged every season. Whitetails range statewide, but are by far most plentiful in the southeast and east. Some top counties: McCurtain, Pushmataha, Cherokee, Atoka, Pittsburg, Osage, Leflore.

The Texas whitetail picture is simply phenomenal, but because of a lease-and-fee system it is not always easy to find a place to hunt, and certainly not free. By far the largest number of whitetails are in the Hill Country, or Edwards Plateau, of south-central Texas. These are of only modest size. Practically every record head, and most trophies, have come out of the so-called Brush Country of southern Texas. There is, however, fair to excellent whitetail hunting practically everywhere in the state.

For a most unusual hunt, try the little Carmen Mountains whitetail, a subspecies that ranges in very modest numbers in small mountain ranges of the Big Bend Country in western Texas. It is a handsome subspecies, often smaller than the Arizona whitetail, but in some respects rather similar. There are big Texas whitetails as well as mule deer in the same terrain. The Texas deer bag limit is high, and on a most interesting hunt several years ago I set out to take a desert mule deer, a Texas whitetail, and a Carmen Mountains whitetail in three days. It was a tough but exciting session and I did succeed.

Western whitetail hunting has been little publicized. The majority of U.S. deer hunters have overlooked it for far too long.

Desert mountains of the Big Bend country in Texas are prime desert mule deer range. Here horsebacking hunters work high ridges at midday.

Desert mule deer are commonly jumped in wide open situations where woodland hunters would hardly believe deer could exist.

CHAPTER 17
HUNTING DESERT MULE DEER

The bases of rimrocks like those at left are prime resting places for desert mule deer.

It was the afternoon before the opening of deer season in the vast, barely populated Big Bend country of far west Texas. Ever since we'd splashed the horses across the trickle of San Francisco Creek, we'd been climbing. I recalled that an old cowpoke from the Big Bend region, when asked where it was, thoughtfully replied, "I reckon it ain't close to nowhere." Pressed for what could possibly be good about it, he said, "It's lonesomer than any place else."

On some Texas maps the area where we were, southeast from the village of Marathon on the huge Gage Holland ranch, is deservingly labeled "Hell's Half Acre." Holland, riding ahead, wanted me to see it and its totally unmolested deer. At that time there were no ranch roads here, no windmills, and thus no cattle. It was a virgin land of ancient desert mountains. Riding into it was like turning the clock back 100 years.

The horses labored up the steep slope, the insecure footing of deep, small rock shards making them slip and plunge. I was musing that when you've hunted deer for several decades, as I had, quite literally coast to coast, border to border and beyond, and in every conceivable habitat they'd managed to colonize, you know emphatically the kind of hunting you most enjoy. If it happens to be, as in my case, desert mule deer, sometimes you wonder *why*.

We topped out and paused to let the horses blow. The view was awesome. Jagged haze-blue mountains hulked southward toward the Rio Grande. The enormous fault called the "Devil's Backbone," with its colossal lizard-scale contours, undulated across the panorama. As we slumped in our saddles, resting, a magnificent buck with massive mahogany antlers appeared skylighted atop the ridge above us. Broadside, it stared down at these strange interlopers in its remote domain.

Musing ceased. Suddenly I knew why I prefer desert hunts to all others. Those blocky, pale-gray deer that make you suffer in settings where deer seem not to belong — they and their surroundings were the reason. Without question this is the most dramatic, intriguing deer hunting extant, a unique challenge. Desert mule deer country, compared to any other deer habitat, is conscienceless, contemptuous of the anguish it may deal the unwary. It's the classic example of "buyer beware." And yet, it's mesmerizing.

My first tenderfoot hunt years earlier had offered a prime example of both. In the mountains south of Tucson, Arizona, I watched a buck ghost through a dense cholla cactus thicket whose countless crooked arms festooned with millions of straw-colored spines appeared impenetrable. The buck came out upon an open rocky slope, framed between two giant saguaros. Desert mule deer were this easy, eh?

I raised my rifle and rested it against the trunk of the shrub screening me. A thorn slit my palm. I jerked back. My right foot struck a piece of what natives call "jumping cholla." It flipped up, the stiff spines pinning it to my calf. In pain, I started to pry it off with the only available tool, my gun barrel. Then, something I saw froze my movement. A rattler lay coiled within strike range. Unaware now of the cholla pain, I eased back. Meanwhile, the buck disappeared over the ridge.

All this doesn't mean desert mule deer country is prohibitively perilous. Those living in it would scoff. After all, many deer ranges have snakes; you could fatally fall from a New England tree stand; break a leg on a Pacific slope; or tangle with a Montana grizzly. Desert settings simply make you pay closer attention — or chance suffering more than elsewhere. To compensate, there are the unique surroundings and the excitement of seeing these splendid animals, evolved from their highly specialized environment, spang out in the open almost every day.

The desert mule deer, *Odocoileus hemionus crooki*, is perhaps the most interesting North American deer. Its range, confined to the continent's harshest deserts, is restricted to southern Arizona and New Mexico, western Texas, and south far into Mexico.

These are animals of the desert floor and mountain foothills. Water is always scarce, except on ranches where windmills or tanks furnish it for cattle. Some naturalists insist that the deer can go for long periods of time with water only from plants. Clumps of low-growing sotol, for example, have a cabbage-like center that desert deer eat for both food and liquid. I've watched them munching juice-filled prickly pear pads, somehow braving the spines. In Arizona I once observed a buck rip apart a stiff-barbed barrel cactus with its antlers, then eat the watery pulp.

When I began this desert hunting, I assumed that the animals would be thin and the meat leather tough. To date I've tagged thirty-odd desert deer, and all were fat and tender. I've eaten venison from throughout the nation and desert mule deer are always the best. They're marvels of adaptation, withstanding weather conditions ranging from 120-degree heat to the occasional bitter cold and snow.

Watching desert muleys utilize sparse cover is a lesson for hunters everywhere. One day on the Holland ranch, Gage and I drove during midday, glassing the open slopes. Only scattered shrubs and cactus broke the vast expenses of sparse ground vegetation. We located eight bucks in 2 hours, each bedded in the spot of shade from a single bush. Daytime thermals rising from valleys warn them of danger below. Stealthy approach from the open slope above is impossible.

Once on such a slope I saw a ten-point buck bound from its bed beside a sotol clump not 2 feet high. It ran up into an area where a half dozen scattered yuccas were the only consequential vegetation. It whirled behind one, dropped flat, and stretched its head and neck out on the ground. On several occasions I've stood glassing bucks as they fed along open ridges. Each stared, moved slowly ahead to the first bayonet, yucca, or cholla, then in slow motion lay down behind the meager cover.

Desert mule deer are somewhat smaller than Rocky Mountain deer. Some biologists believe the scientific rule applies that animals in hot regions have lesser body mass in relation to surface area in order to more efficiently dispel heat. Most big bucks I've taken weighed 140 to 170 pounds field dressed. The largest, shot on Holland's place during one of the dozen seasons I've hunted there, field dressed 195.

Desert mule deer are paler than their mountain relatives. The dark brow area is also lighter and smaller. The antlers often lack brow tines, or have comparatively small ones. The tail may have a faint black stripe down its base.

It's true that the measurements of maximum-sized antlers are less for desert deer. One reason, little known among hunters, is that all skull measurements of this subspecies are also smaller than those of the mountain type. Nonetheless, antlers of adult desert bucks reach gratifying proportions. I've shot several with 22 to 24 inch spreads, and seen one of 28 and another of 30. However, a look at any eight- or ten-point buck in this wide-open country is guaranteed to make a hunter quiver.

That gets us to one really important focus of this hunting. It *isn't* often record oriented. That's one reason it's so enjoyable. Coping with desert surroundings, and the delights of watching and hunting deer in this incongruous habitat are the others. I vividly remember a day when Gage Holland and I drove in a 4 × 4 all day on his enormous spread. We didn't hunt; we watched, glassed, and photographed deer, counting over 100. I still see in my mind's eye a photo that I couldn't get — seven eight- and ten-point bucks posed together on a bald rocky hummock a few hundred yards away.

That image suggests easy hunting, and in truth, many Texans do have it so. Success also is highest here. That's because hunting is done almost entirely on private lands — ranches of a few thousand to a hundred thousand or more acres. Deer, and hunter numbers, are carefully managed. Most hunting is done by vehicle — glassing the foothills — and thus covering much territory. Walking is in brief stalks or scouts of canyons and deep washes. A few ranches offer horseback hunts.

On Texas' public lands, and on a few ranches where season leases can be acquired, hunters do it the hard way — they walk. This approach is standard in New Mexico and Arizona on the vast public lands where vehicle trails are scarce. An indication of how difficult this hunting is can be seen in Arizona's harvest figures. In that state the desert mule deer kill and that of the extremely wary little Coues whitetail often run about equal, or even higher for the whitetail.

These figures are also indicative of the comparatively small number of sportsmen who hunt desert mule deer. The Texas hunter total is also low. Ranchers who charge fees keep the numbers in check. The modest number of hunters throughout the range points to a further delight: hunting is never crowded.

Occasionally you wish that you had others with whom to share your misery. A southeastern Arizona hunt I made years ago in the Chiricahua foothills presented a wryly amusing vignette of desert deer and desert coping. The guide was a whitebearded former cowpoke, the alleged cook was his buddy. In those years this was primitive country. We headquartered in a dirt-floored 'dobe shack and would make bets on who'd win the nightly scorpion kill pot. The cook worked one-handed over an outdoor fire while his free hand gripped the neck of a tequila bottle. I marveled that he never fell in the fire and avoided asking what it was he served, figuring I was better off not knowing.

We walked the slopes, ridges, and draws, and climbed the rimrocks. Those are prime bedding places, with spots of shade available in giant crevices. It was hot — just right for snakes. We climbed warily.

Desert vegetation and rocks are the chief annoyances hunters in this country fight. If you think southwestern desert-mountain country has sand underfoot, think again. Sharp-edged rock rubble litters slopes, covers ridges, and often the desert floor, as well. Boots must be tough. I was then only mildly desert experienced. By the end of the second day my feet and legs were killing me.

Vegetation is perhaps your worst enemy. If you horseback, you'll need leather chaps. If you walk, tough brush pants are mandatory. None were then available. Short catclaw thorns shredded my clothes. My hands had several thorns buried in them, along with the hair-fine cactus spines you can't see but feel at every move. Virtually every desert plant waits either to stick you or stab you.

Lechugilla is a particularly vicious species. It grows in patches among rocky ground cover on slopes. The plants, which grow densely close together, reach about a foot high. A whorl of upright thick, stiff leaves with knife-like points invites disaster. Deer dig them out and eat the juicy leaf bases. I walked across a patch and badly sliced one leg. Nail-like thorns of low ground mesquite pierced one boot sole.

The comic relief came at third-day dawn. Cookie sat on a rock by his fire, awesomely hung over, and loudly complaining about the pain in his feet. He wore old pointy-toed cowboy boots — and had each on the wrong foot! Even with this corrected, he still wailed about violent pain in his left big toe. He'd forgotten to shake out his boots, a morning ritual in such places, and a squashed scorpion that had stung him before its death was stuck to his sock. That morning I shot a forkhorn near camp, an excuse for getting out of there.

Over the years I learned the ways of the desert, which any desert mule deer hunter would be wise to do. The preponderance of my hunts in Texas have been less painful. The more I chased desert mule deer, the more they mesmerized me and the more the desert mountains enchanted me. If I were to select a hunt that rates as the most memorable, it would be one on Gage Holland's place.

Some 20 ranch-road miles from headquarters there was a huge butte-like rock pile that heaved up from a broad flat. At daylight you would often find deer on the flats or on lower slopes. By midmorning most have moved up to bed beside a bush, under a rim, or among the enormous rock chunks atop the upthrust. Holland knew I was familiar with the place.

He told me, "There's a ten-point that lives around that hump with the biggest body I've seen this year."

About midday I started the steep climb. Even in December the day was a scorcher, and the 4,000-plus altitude had me winded. I rested briefly, then stealthily padded across, jumping narrow breaks. Rattling shale brought me up short with my rifle unslung. I couldn't see the buck until it hit the flat running all out. I'd botched it, and I wouldn't try a tail-on running shot.

Disgruntled, I muttered epithets at the deer. Apparently that helped. The deer stopped and turned broadside. It was too far away, though; I guessed its distance from me to be perhaps 375 yards. I hunkered down and laid my left hand palm up on a rock, with my .264

barrel across it. Temptation nudged. I held midway on the ribs, compensating for the steep downward angle. The bullet struck the buck just below the backbone.

It was the heavy deer Gage had seen, and the largest desert deer in antlers and weight I've ever tagged. I had the head mounted and presented it to Holland. It still graces a ranch headquarters wall.

Author drags excellent 8-point Carmen Mts. whitetail from kill site to vehicle. This is the U.S.' rarest huntable whitetail.

Diminutive Carmen Mts. deer are found in the U.S. only in a few small mountain ranges of far west Texas, where these hunters work a mountain side.

CHAPTER 18

THE MINIATURE WHITETAIL

My first Carmen Mts. whitetail buck. It
weighed, field dressed, only 45 pounds.

Somehow it seems appropriate that anything rare should be small and lent appeal by its miniature size. The concept certainly holds true for the Carmen Mountains whitetail deer. An adult buck that weighs 75 pounds field-dressed is a cracking good one, and one of 100 pounds is a monster. The Carmen Mountains whitetail is in fact the smallest legally huntable whitetail within U.S. boundaries, slightly smaller on the average than the Coues whitetail of Arizona and New Mexico. Only the fully protected Key deer of the Florida Keys is smaller.

One of my most dramatic deer hunting memories concerns these tiny Carmen Mountains deer. There were two bucks, both excellent trophies. They looked positively huge because what I was seeing was not the actual deer but the projection of their racing, vastly magnified shadows thrown by a low sun upon a pale, vertical wall of rock. It was a most unusual and stirring scene, never to be forgotten.

The place was an enormous ranch in Brewster County, Texas, a tremendous expanse of desert and mountains in what is called the Big Bend Country. I was coming down out of a steep, narrow canyon called Doubtful, because it is often doubtful that one can get in or out of it! The two bucks must have been moving casually along a low rim on my right when I unwittingly startled them. Suddenly on my left I was conscious of motion. Probably sun and rock and deer could never again be placed so that such a phenomenon might occur. I turned swiftly left, raising my rifle. Two gigantic black deer, perfectly outlined, antlers showing in full detail, flags flying, were racing along the face of the vertical rock wall.

With reflexive action I had the rifle against my shoulder, then felt foolish because it was instantly obvious that I was chasing shadows. They were so exquisitely perfect, the motion swift and fluid as they flitted across the rock wall. I turned frantically right, trying to catch a glimpse of the real bucks and hoping for a shot. But they were gone.

I realized I was shaking, and I chuckled, sheepish but still filled with the thrill of the scene, those towering, black, bucks' shadows in my mind's eye still racing across the face of the pale cliff. I moved on down doubtful, heart still thumping, reflecting that the total life experience of a hunter is a collection of many such art-oriented happenings that can never be repeated.

The range of the Carmen Mountains whitetail, one of the 17 subspecies of whitetails found within U.S. borders, spreads over Brewster and a couple of its neighboring counties and reaches south of the border into the Sierra del Carmen, for which it is named, in the Mexican state of Coahuila.

It is scattered in relatively small pockets in the high, timbered desert-mountain ranch country where pinyon, madrona and oak grow in the numerous small mountain ranges of this region of Texas. Excepting the Key deer and several whitetail subspecies restricted to islands along our Atlantic coast, the Carmen Mountains whitetail has the smallest range of any whitetail variety within the U.S. Its status as rarest huntable U.S. whitetail rests on the fact that, according to a recent survey, probably not more than 1500-2000 of the animals are found within our borders. However, this deer is by no means an endangered or threatened species.

The Carmen Mountains whitetail is commonly spoken of in western Texas as a "flag" or "flagtail." This name generally is intended to differentiate between it and the standard Texas whitetail subspecies, the common and much larger whitetail that blankets most of the state. To one seeing it for the first time as it flees, the tail appears out of all proportion. The illusion is caused by the fact that the tail is broadly fringed with white along the edges of the top as well as beneath. This extra-long white hair, which also runs down the inside of the back legs, makes the upraised tail appear longer and broader than it is.

The top side of the tail is also an important key to identification. In pure specimens it is cinnamon buff or rusty reddish down the center, usually edged with darker hair in a blackish-brown hue. Overall, the Carmen Mountains deer is grizzled gray, not the smooth gray-to-brownish of most other whitetails. A close examination shows the individual hairs banded with black and white, producing the distinctly grizzled appearance. The ears are longer in relation to overall body size than those of the Texas whitetail, but somewhat shorter than those of the Coues or Arizona whitetail with which it is often confused. The antlers are distinctive, with tines much shorter than those of the average Texas whitetail. The main beams usually swing well around forward, snug and basket-like.

The reason I describe this deer in some detail is that there are Texas whitetails in the same mountain ranges. They are, of course, larger, and as a rule they are found in the foothills, whereas many Carmen Mountains deer range as high up as the country reaches, into the thick stands of timber and brush atop the mountains. There are also many desert mule deer in the same terrain, but these are chiefly down on the desert floor and on foothill slopes.

Because both the Texas whitetail and the Carmen Mountains whitetail dwell on the same range, interbreeding between the two is common. I have seen big, burly whitetails with the grizzled color of the little Carmen deer, and sometimes the top of the tail is a mixed blackish-brown and rusty. This is why there is no trophy class for the Carmen Mountains deer in the record book, as there is for the Coues. The Coues has no other U.S. whitetail subspecies with which to interbreed, but trying to judge whether or not a head from a Carmen Mountains buck was totally pure strain would be next to impossible.

Nonetheless, when one is in their range, atop the mountains, the chance of running into crosses is not high. It is easy for a practiced eye, experienced with the small deer, to recognize them instantly. The snug rack, with short tines, and the miniature size of adult bucks is a quick giveaway. They're so exasperatingly elusive, however, that hunting often can be frustrating. You catch glimpses, as if they truly were ghosts of the desert mountains.

The fronts and sides of the legs of this subspecies are colored a curious red-brown. The color has even been described scientifically as "pinkish buff." Usually the grizzled quality is present, too. Occasionally reddish overall color phases of the flagtail occur. I was hunting one time with Jim Barbee on a ranch a few miles north of Alpine, Texas, when he collected a trophy doe that I greatly envied.

Barbee, who is a mule deer guide, is a fantastic shot. Yet I've never seen anyone — even him — shoot as he did that day. We were walking a high canyon bottom early in the afternoon of an overly warm December day. He suddenly whirled to his right, having seen motion high on the slope. His gun was coming up as he pivoted. I never saw the deer, but at the shot he yelled, "Got 'im!" As he said it, he was swinging his gun again. At that instant his boot slipped. He fell flat, jumped up, shot with unbelievable speed, and yelped, "Got 'em both!"

I couldn't imagine what he'd been shooting at. It turned out he'd spotted two flagtails, a buck and a doe, just as they spooked and ran. The range was at least 200 yards up the steep slope. He had killed both notwithstanding his fall. Under permits he held, both were of course legal. When we climbed up to bring them down, we discovered he had a handsome little eight-point, gray-grizzled buck, and an unbelievably rare doe. She was glossy, pale cinnamon all over — body, legs, and head.

I talked later with Tommy Hailey, a Texas game department employee who had done a study of these deer. He told me he had seen a few with this curious color phase. It was one of the most handsome deer I've ever seen. But as it turned out, for some reason or another, we never took a single photo of it.

For years there has been confusion about the Carmen Mountains whitetail in Texas. Many experienced hunters still insist, ridiculously, that it is the Coues deer. However, a check of the record book will show that no Coues has ever been accepted from Texas — for very good reason. The range of the Coues does not extend east in New Mexico past the north-south line of the Rio Grande River. To further confuse the matter, the range of the Carmen Mountains deer, usually above 5,000 feet in a region where the highest peaks run up not quite to 8,000, is kind of a series of small islands totally surrounded by the range of the Texas whitetail.

Curiously, landowners in the region are not at all fond of the little whitetails, or of any whitetails for that matter. The game department has to some extent encouraged this dislike. This area, ranchers claim, is mule deer country. The desert mule deer which live here are handsome animals, have long been abundant, and are an extremely important money crop for landowners. Hunters pay high fees to hunt them, for mule deer range in Texas is rather limited. Whitetails — the Texas whitetail — both game department and ranchers claim have been increasing in west-Texas mule deer country, crowding out mule deer. Whether or not this is true, the mule deer are having difficulties, even though hunting is still excellent. Landowners like to get rid of the whitetails, of whatever subspecies. A few, it is suspected, kill them on sight just to rid their range of them.

Setting up a Carmen Mountains whitetail hunt is tough. Landowners and guides in the area obviously don't object to hunters taking the little whitetails. But the animals are exasperatingly difficult to hunt because the cover is dense in their favored habitat. It is also rugged. And, the deer are maddeningly shy and spooky. No guide wants to take time during the brief mule deer season to bother with this hunting when he can so much more easily fill mule deer tags for his clients.

One method I found that works rather well and presents the right psychology is to book a two-deer hunt. Only one buck mule deer is legal anyway. So, you have an understanding with a guide or landowner that you are mule deer hunting, but if you get a chance at a flagtail you are allowed to take it — and pay, of course. Or, you keep an eye out while hunting mule deer, try to fill your mule deer tag quickly, then go flagtail hunting. This gives the guide or landowner a chance to make a profit, and you are helping them by taking the whitetails, which they don't want anyway.

Another approach is to try to set up a strictly whitetail hunt. I hunted on one ranch last year where there were possibly 40 hunters, and the owner had asked that they all cooperate in taking whitetails instead of mule deer if at all possible to help balance the herd. Because it is legal to take two whitetail bucks, the hunter who agrees to try to do so, and doesn't argue about price unduly, may find he'll get some takers.

For those who wish to try flagtail hunting, it must be realized that distribution is spotty. You have to study the terrain and hunt above 5000 feet in the timber. The combination of pinyon, oak and madrona has in my experience always held the majority of these deer. Further, you have to hunt as high up as possible to get away from most of the mule deer and the majority of the Texas whitetails.

The three counties with the most flagtails are Brewster, Presidio and Jeff Davis. The larger towns in the area are Marfa, Alpine and Ft. Davis. Chambers of commerce in these towns may be able to help. The fellow who states that he wants to bag a couple of whitetails is likely to be more welcome as the years advance. In my experience, the greatest abundance of flagtails is south of U.S. 90, and the farther down toward Big Bend Park the better. This probably will all be private land. To my knowledge, at least, there is no public west-Texas hunting land where flagtails are resident.

I remember with amusement a little flagtail buck I collected a few years ago on a morning when the west-Texas sunshine was of the sort in which you could drown. An old ranch hand was guiding me when we spotted a deer across a ridge just out of range. It was barely dawn with fog thicker than chowder and rain pouring through it as if through a strainer. The buck was hunched disconsolately under a drooping, dripping Gambel's oak, and it didn't look much bigger than a jackrabbit.

I said to the guide, "That's the smallest buck I've ever seen. I don't want to fool with it."

"How many days you been trying to collect one of those miserable little deer?" he asked.

"Three." I answered.

"How many days you got to hunt?"

"This is the last."

He took the lid off a snuff can, sculptured a big wad and stuffed it into his lip. "If you got much sense," he said, "you'll see if you kin shoot that deer. Seems like you'd realize by now they ain't easy."

It began to dawn on me maybe he was right. The rain was harder now. I slipped along the trail, trying to keep my scope covered. The overcast was so thick it was almost evening dark. The little buck stood under the drooping oak, rain running down its plump sides. It had four points, and I knew darned well it wouldn't weigh 50 pounds field-dressed. I slid off the safety and knelt behind a bush. Seconds later the hunt was over.

"You reckon you can carry your own deer back to the pickup?" the guide asked. "Cain't be more'n 50 yards." He wiped rain drippings off his nose.

"I can manage it," I said.

It was indeed small, but a perfectly beautiful little buck, its grizzled sides plump and glossy. I picked up the buck and swung it over my shoulder. We stood and laughed together, rain running off us.

"Typewriter sure keeps you guys' muscles in shape," the old ranch hand said. "Don't stagger under the weight."

We plodded back to the crotchety pickup and argued with it to get it started. At headquarters we weighed the buck on an old spring scale. Forty-five pounds. I was thinking, reading the scale, that most deer hunters brag how big, not how little. Indeed it is true, anything rare should be in miniature, and thus provocatively appealing. The Carmen Mountains whitetail is positive proof.

In the Texas Hill Country this buck was discovered living in a small patch of woods surrounded by farm fields.

In areas of small farms many a good buck keeps its presence secret by hiding in small woodlots, or even in unharvested crop fields. This one had been overlooked for several seasons, but tracks gave it away.

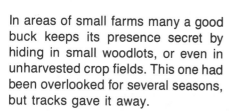

CHAPTER 19
PRIME WHITETAIL BUCKS
YOU OVERLOOK

This good buck spent its days in an inconsequential appearing patch of brush where most hunters would never look.

Every whitetail deer hunter entertains pre-hunt dreams of downing a trophy buck. But of the more than 1 ½ million whitetails harvested each year, statistics show that 90 percent of the bucks are so-so specimens and, nationwide, fewer than one hunter in five fills a tag of any kind, buck or doe.

Why isn't the success ratio higher? Why aren't more big bucks bagged? The answer is simple: Hunters just aren't sharp enough at *seeing* cover-loving whitetails. Even most misses are caused because a deer wasn't spotted soon enough.

Recently, Tom Hennessey, a rancher friend of mine, was discussing this. Tom owns a big place and takes fifty-odd hunters every fall, in some of the best whitetail range on the continent. He was talking about the countless tales of deer collected and bigger ones not collected to which he is annually subjected throughout our six-week season.

"For years," Tom told me, "I've kept a log of hunter stories, by categories. It tells some interesting tales of its own. A certain type of hunter tries new places each season, is always dissatisfied because he never sees many deer. Some others seldom see bucks, but do see numerous does and fawns. Lots fail to see big bucks at all. Many don't see 'the big one' quickly enough. Only a few regularly bring in trophies."

Tom knows the deer on his place like he knows his cattle. He told of an exceptional buck he had watched for four years. It lived in the vicinity of a waterhole surrounded by dense cover, in the middle of a pasture of 1 square mile.

"Every hunter I assigned there I told about that buck. It was an unusually fine six-pointer the first year I noticed it, a heavy-horned nine the next, a near-record ten the last two. Of twenty hunters I put in there over the four years, only three ever saw it. One almost stepped on it as the old boy lay doggo in its bed hoping he'd pass. Scared the hunter witless. Another realized too late he was looking at it through a screen of brush. The third was a trophy hunter with a string of big whitetails behind him. He killed it."

"How?"

"He didn't *hunt*. He spent three days just *looking*, watching the waterhole area from 150 yards off. Never went near it. Told me he was interested only in the first hour of dawn and the last hour of shooting light. But he got settled in long before daylight, and again by mid-afternoon, so as not to disturb things. Just glassed that small area incessantly. He never did see the whole deer until he walked up on it dead. In almost the last light of the third afternoon he located with his glass two heavy antler tips wide apart in the brush, a wet nose with some shine, and just enough neck in the clear to shoot at. It didn't make the book, but it came close."

Hennessey's story can be valuable to any whitetail hunter hoping to improve his score. First, you have to learn more about *how to look*. Second, you must realize there are three kinds of whitetail hunting: the extra-tough kind, for big bucks; the moderately difficult kind, for so-so bucks; the easiest operation, for antlerless deer. If you're seeing numerous does and fawns (except during the rut), you aren't hunting or looking where the big bucks are. Third, you have to be a much sharper "looker" for the big one than for the little one. Fourth, patience and perseverance in looking, and a quality binocular, are mandatory. Three-fourths of the time afield should be spent using eyes and glass, Hennessey claims, and no more than one-fourth "hunting," as the average hunter understands that term.

Much of the "looking" shortcomings stem from the way hunters imagine they'll see the trophy, or at least the way they'd *like* to see it — spang in the open, close, broadside, immobile, undisturbed. This can happen, of course. But it rarely does, and with old bucks almost never. For every whitetail that's easy to see, dozens remain unseen. Does, commonly seen in moderately open places (unless you're after one) should be a warning. Get away from them. They're tattletale nuisances — again, excepting some lone does during the rut. Bucks, especially mature bucks, should be thought of as totally different animals compared to does. They're far more secretive, seldom curious, always more difficult to see because they try harder to keep from being seen.

Much has been written about never looking for a whole deer. It's the best possible advice. Scan cover meticulously for opposing or unnatural lines: the softly curved horizontal line of the back; two, or four, sapling trunks placed too symmetrically that become deer legs after long scrutiny; the upslanting curve of the neck; part of the curve of an antler; the rounded-triangle tip of an ear. Glue an eye to that. It's the one part of an immobile deer that's most likely to move. Observe, too, that outlines of portions of deer in cover are rounded, the lines softer than the more severe geometrics of brush and timber.

Here are some other looking clues. A deer facing or with head turned toward you shows the pale bone-white throat area, a wholly unnatural shade and design among a crisscross of cover. The nose pad, licked intermittently, is black and shines slightly even in dim light. If you suspect you're seeing this even with all the rest of the head screened by cover, look immediately below for the off-white tip of the lower jaw. Look also for a similar shade in small spots below and to the side of each nostril, and for the broken circle of off-white on the snout immediately behind the nose pad. Study any suspected deer part, no matter how small, long and carefully. You may suddenly begin to see the entire outline.

Whole antlers seldom show, but the color of antlers on vigorous bucks is dark tan to mahogany, and parts of them shine whenever light touches them through dappled sun and shade. Over-the-hill bucks, those less vigorous, those that started antlers in poor growing seasons, have whitish antlers, often with little or no shine. No one — no one — should plan on seeing, or keep looking for, a whitetail buck whole or in the open. Concentrate on looking for bits and pieces in cover. If by unusual luck you do happen to see the whole deer, you'll know it!

Keep in mind, too, that parts of a deer, antlers included, do *not* look exactly like parts of the woods cover containing them. Hunters are fond of claiming (excuses, excuses!) that they match inseparably. The fact is that to the astute observer, nothing animal, and alive, looks precisely like anything in the plant world, or anything dead. Hunters are also fond of claiming the big one was in brush too dense to shoot through. To the close observer this is seldom true. A good scope, particularly a variable cranked up to high power for the moment, can usually discover a hole if the shooter remains calm and unhurried. After all, a bullet requires only a small, lethally located patch of target plus an inconsequential opening between twigs.

A friend of mine who has hunted whitetails for fifty years has an additional and interesting psychological approach to looking that he backs up with intriguing statistics. "A fellow certainly can get himself into a situation where there are no deer, or few. But most hunters, if they observe sign properly, are surrounded by at least some deer, wherever they hunt. You should always *assume* you are in their presence, and act in accordance, not just timidly hope you may be. That keeps you alert and looking properly."

His backup proof concerns the fact that game managers, on the average, plan to harvest no more than 10 percent of an existing herd. The sex ratio of whitetails runs roughly 52 percent bucks, 48 percent does. Granted, bucks receive the most concentrated hunter attention. So, as the season ends, there are still probably seven or eight bucks, several real trophies, and nine or ten does left in the woods for every one that became venison. If you didn't see them, think about that!

One of the most intriguing bits of lore regarding how to look for whitetails was discovered inadvertently when I had a telephoto camera rather than a gun in my hands. I knew well that bucks, even the smaller ones, spend most of the daylight hours in heavy cover. If I wanted to get photos during the day, just as in hunting, I'd have to go into the thickets with utmost care and silence. An advantage for the hunter, I had long ago discovered, is that trophy bucks particularly are loathe to give themselves away by moving. They often stay absolutely still, hoping you will not discover them.

The big disadvantage for a photographer in cover, I soon found, was that light was very dim for photos, or else an impossible hodge-podge of light and shadow. With the light behind me or high over a shoulder, where I tried to keep it so I'd have all that was available on the subject, it was extremely difficult for either my eye or my camera to get enough contrast to see an image that didn't simply meld with the background.

There was a certain expanse of mixed cedar and oak with small growth underneath where I knew a big buck hung out. On this day the small breeze was coming from the sun direction. Therefore I was forced, unhappily, to move toward the light. Any subject ahead of me would be backlighted, but to my amazement, I spotted the buck easily.

There were shafts of light falling here and there through the trees onto small patches of pale understory grass. I suddenly realized the antlers and head of the buck were perfectly silhouetted against one of these. Since then I have hunted with both rifle and camera in resting cover for deer during the mid-morning to late-afternoon hours, always moving *against* the light, even when it is almost overhead.

Deer do not lie down all the time while resting in cover. You are as likely to find a trophy buck standing as bedded. Except on overcast days, hunting against the light in cover during deer rest periods will allow you to pick out bits and pieces of your quarry far more efficiently.

One aspect of learning to see whitetails better that has hardly been touched is reversing the viewpoint. How does the deer do its looking? Knowledge of the physical attributes of a deer's eye is enlightening, and teaches you much about what it sees and about its preferences in light intensity.

Deer are color blind. Far from being a handicap, this probably has advantages for them. The fall woods, for example, can actually be confusing to the human eye, which tries to sort out from its welter of colors the drab bits and pieces of deer we look for. Conversely, the deer, living in a world of gray, sees unnatural shapes and hues that are in contrast to its surroundings and that may mean danger.

The eye of a deer lacks the cone cells that receive the varied wave lengths of light that form the color spectrum. But it is far better equipped than ours with rod cells, the ones that interpret the shades of gray and take over in colorless fading light. There are millions more of these cells than in the human eye. This is why a deer's eye reflects light at night and a human eye doesn't.

These cells make it possible for deer to see well at night, even in the most meager light, perhaps only from the glow of a few stars. In fact, this indicates something extremely important to the hunter: It is a creature of low-light preferences, tilted even toward being nocturnal. Its movements are heavily influenced by dim light. The older and wiser a buck becomes, the more it clings to the dim recesses of heavy cover when light is high, and the more it moves at night or during the lowest light levels.

Therefore, the earliest and latest possible shooting light periods are the best times to find trophy bucks active. I have kept track of the fairly numerous good to excellent whitetail bucks I've killed over my forty-odd years of hunting. Not one was taken out in bright places during the day. Several were stalked in dark cover in daytime, a tricky, slow-motion, seldom-successful business. All the rest were shot at dawn or dusk.

Do not take too literally the statement that whitetail bucks are most "active" very early and very late. All too many hunters expect to see bucks actually *moving* during these hours. They sit and watch for movement, and some, to be sure, are successful. All too often, however, there is little or no visible movement. The old buck cautiously peers out from the darkness of cover for long minutes before coming to the edge.

One of the biggest whitetails I ever missed out on did exactly this. I had been studying a cedar brake edge from about 100 yards off for an hour as light waned. Tiring, and admittedly somewhat bored, I put down my glass and closed my eyes momentarily. When I lifted it again, something way back under the dark cedars looked different. It slowly came into focus as a buck so big as to make you quit breathing. It was not even near the edge, but stood with head low, far back in the trees, casing the edge and open outside area.

The light was almost gone. In my haste to put down the glass and raise my rifle, I clinked a rock. In the evening stillness that was enough. The deer didn't run. It simply faded back into the cover, and probably waited for full dark before venturing forth.

The lesson to be learned is that when light changes drastically, deer are more wary and uneasy than at any other time. At dawn, the light quickly sweeps away the safety of darkness. And during the fading of light late in the day, deer venture nervously from safe hiding places into edges and openings where dangers may have become ensconced during the time the animals were absent from them. Crafty old bucks stand and stare out interminably, making absolutely certain of safety before they move. Indeed, they may not come into the open edge at all until dark.

The only way to see them is by glassing intently with the same tireless diligence they evidence in their looking. The average hunter, I suspect, doesn't really know what patient and meticulous glassing means. You don't just sweep a glass around. In fact, you don't sweep it at all. You study yard by yard, assuming a deer is somewhere in the scene. You don't sit for just 5 minutes. You get comfortable, conceal-ed at a likely viewing point, knees up and elbows planted on them, and work with a glass for a full hour.

You keep in mind that whitetails in cover invariably take advan-tage of shadows, which must be studied more closely than the bright spots. You check for long periods areas of contrasting light and shadow, which are camouflage to a deer yet may show glints or mere flickers of movement in the lighted pockets. And in the lowest light, when there are no contrasts at all, you seek animate but not necessarily animated shapes — a front end, a rear end, a body barrel, a head with ears cocked and listening.

There is a busy guide I know, a close friend who squeezes me in a short whitetail hunt most seasons. He is the classic example of what looking for bucks is all about. There's no use to name him, because he stays booked up several years ahead. The reason is that he invariably finds big bucks for his clients. I have to admit he nearly drives me up the canyon wall with his interminable glassing.

One hunt was typical. We were in brush and cactus country near the Mexican border, on 30,000 acres of rugged range teeming with deer, and we were the only hunters for two days. This type of whitetail habitat, in which I have often hunted, is, in my estimation, the most difficult in existence — awesomely dense and exasperatingly feature-less. I suppose we could have driven around and run up a buck somewhere. But that's not the way this gent does it.

We drove out a mile or so from camp at mid-morning and stopped to look at a ridge and then at the jumbled canyon laced by thornbrush and rock that it overlooked. "Bound to be a big deer down there," he said. "Let's go find him." He started up the ridge.

Below the ridge crest, screened by a few bushes, we hunkered down. He piled up several rocks and laid our jackets across them. "There's your rest," he said. He was assuming a lot!

An hour later I was almost dozing, having combed the canyon endlessly with my own binocular and finally given up. I really wanted to leave, but he was still at it. Forty-five minutes later I suddenly realized that for long minutes his glass hadn't changed position.

Finally, without taking the binocular off target, he said. "All right. I've found your deer. Crank your scope up to 9X and look where I'm looking. There's a mountain laurel bush by itself, and a big gray rock 10 feet to the right. The deer's bedded in the shadow of the rock, in some bushes. His neck near the shoulder is clear. Big rack but hard to see."

It took me some time. With adrenalin rising, I probed the area, finally found bush and rock. Nothing else. Then suddenly the image began to fill in line by line. I was looking at a buck that later proved to be a whopping ten-pointer.

That highly successful guide says it all succinctly: "Pick a place that seems likely for a big buck. Assume there's a deer in it and that this is a puzzle you're working to find it. Never mind how long it takes. Stay at least an hour or two. Get so you can see the big ones, and you won't have to worry about the little ones!"

Author with Carmen Mts. whitetail buck, the rarest and smallest huntable
North American deer.

Fine whitetail buck moving during midday, a time few hunters utilize, but should.

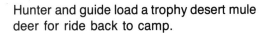
Hunter and guide load a trophy desert mule deer for ride back to camp.

Arid country hunting can be hot at midday. Hunter pauses at waterhole to cool face and neck.

Guide Jim Barbee, left, has author's son Terry use his hat for a soft rest atop boulder, to avoid jar that might influence trajectory.

Hunter glasses from top of slope. A binocular is a must for any deer hunter.

Author moves in to tag an excellent Rocky Mt. mule deer, among aspens in Utah high country.

Hunter takes quick aim at desert mule deer in the southwest.

Author, right, and Ted Burt of the New Mexico game department, use spotting scope to search for trophy Rocky Mt. mule deer.

Bucks like this one are easily spooked. When one looks toward your stand, keep your face down and remain immobile until its attention wavers.

Nowadays tree stands, ready-made or like this one, and also high, commercially built seats, are exceedingly popular. They're a great assistance, but you must be quiet. Deer may not look up at sharp angles, but can distantly spot you.

CHAPTER 20
SITTING FOR DEER

One of the most important aspects of selecting a sitting place is making sure it's comfortable, so you can be completely still.

Reams have been written about how to still hunt for deer and how to prowl the woods most effectively. Little is said, however, about how to be a successful stand sitter. Mention of it even sounds kind of silly. It's not. Sitting still is as much an art, with its own rules and techniques, as still-hunting.

I had the occasion to teach one of my grandsons how to sit quietly when I took him on his first stand. I had helped him get started as a deer hunter and was ready to help him in this next step. During his first trials, I sat with him. As a youngster, he couldn't be expected to walk quietly enough just yet, and throughout those first hunts I shushed and prompted endlessly. A year later I stashed him in a blind on our ranch and, to see how he would do, left him for the first time on his own.

The blind was a wooden boxlike shelter painted dark green. It had a door and roof and was open at the rear for access. The other three sides were boarded up, except for an open section 18 inches high that ran around the blind at sighting level. The view through the sighting-level slit was blocked only at the corners by the posts. The hunter sat on a plank placed on horizontal braces. From his seat he had a good view along a partially open ridge straight ahead and could see portions of valley approaches on either side.

I didn't tell my grandson when I left what I intended to do. I moved off about 70 yards and hunkered beneath an oak. The morning was very still. I listened intently, thinking of myself as a deer moving in the vicinity. After 1½ hours I figured he'd had about all the sitting he could take, and I went after him.

"How'd it go?" I asked. He hadn't seen anything. "Did you hear anything?" He shook his head. I said, "I did. You coughed three times, banged your gun barrel against the roof or corner posts twice, cleared your throat — and I bet you didn't even realize you nervously tapped your boot toes on the floor every few minutes." Kind of mean of Ol' Grandad, but a penetrating lesson nonetheless. Nowdays he does his sitting as quietly as can be.

As I pointed out to him, the sounds he made didn't necessarily spook deer in the vicinity. There were no other hunters on the ranch, and the deer were undisturbed. Yet those sounds may have alerted deer intent on crossing the ridge, and cautious animals that they are, may have perhaps turned them on a more circuitous route farther from the origin of the sounds.

Indeed, deer that hear small — and possibly to them unidentified — noises aren't going to run wildly away in panic. But they will be alerted to something unknown, and they certainly aren't going to investigate. During periods of heavy hunting pressure, the large number of hunters thrashing about an area creates a wide variety of unusual noises — which makes deer more reluctant to move about. A hunter on stand at this time cannot afford to add to the already high noise levels.

"Stillness" has many facets, some of which are not readily apparent. What you wear is one of the most important aspects, yet is often the least considered. Much modern hunting clothing, though warm, comfortable, and attractive in appearance, is an abominable nuisance on a deer stand. Nylon outer shells are the standard culprits. I have a dandy down jacket that is a classic noise maker. One year I experimented to find out how far away deer could hear the rustling of its nylon outer shell.

I hunt the deer that reside on my ranch, but those animals that live close to my house are not hunted. Instead, I feed them. If you put food out at about the same time each day, the animals quickly learn when it's feeding time. I made my feeding round, then hid in cedars fifty steps from one location. A few minutes later three deer moved in. I let them get settled down, then moved one sleeve against the side of the jacket. At the minor *swish* every deer raised its head. A few minutes later, I moved my back against some cedar branches. Same result. After several more brushes of nylon against nylon, the deer became nervous. They didn't run, but slowly and reluctantly walked away.

With a breeze present, or at a greater distance, I doubt the clothing sound would be picked up by deer. But the worst effect of noisy clothing is that it inhibits the *hunter's* hearing. Each slow turn of the head produces a scraping rustle, blotting out sounds you may be straining after. Granted, you may be required by law in many states to wear a certain number of square inches of hunter orange; when you select the material, try to get something as soft and noiseless as possible.

I have found that the quietest material for the stand sitter is wool or flannel. Garments made with these fabrics are the quietest of all. Most camouflage suit and coverall materials are made of cottons or blends, which are almost as quiet as wool. Canvas jackets are noisy, but if washed or cleaned a few times are not too objectionable on a stand. A plus is a soft corduroy collar, which cuts down on noise that, when you turn your head, may interfere with your own hearing. If a noisy jacket doesn't have such a collar, have one put on.

If you worry that deer will see and be disturbed by colors, wool shirts or jackets can be chosen in subdued colors. I realize that deer vision is a point of controversy; nevertheless, after slightly more than fifty years of deer hunting, I don't pay much attention to clothing color and deer vision.

There are exceptions. A bright yellow coat in contrast against a dark green stand of pines certainly might alert deer. Contrast and intensity, not color as such, are to blame. A red-and-black checked wool shirt won't even draw a look, *if you sit still*. Years ago I sat many a day on stands in the balsam, poplar, and birch forest of the Great Lakes region. The ground was covered with snow, and I wore a bright red, heavy wool hunting coat. Yet I killed a number of deer within fifty steps and had many more pass me at closer range unaware of my presence.

The important consideration is to at least partially blend into your surroundings. You don't want to stand out in sharp contrast. Assuming that deer do have at least low-level color vision, red against dark green will blend well enough. Or, assuming that they are color blind, the red will be a shade of gray. A dark green camo suit can quickly attract attention if you sit in pale-hued dead grass. Likewise, sand-colored camo might call attention just as quickly if posed against the dark trunk of a tree.

What you wear under the outer garments can be important, too. The fit of shirt and pants need consideration. The expert stand sitter strives for total comfort, so he's relaxed and won't be moving around. A rather comical experience I had while on stand with a friend illustrates the point. My friend was an experienced sitter, but on that morning was wearing a new and too-snug pair of undershorts. Every few minutes he'd mutter in a whisper and attempt to rearrange his uncomfortable shorts. At long last, just as he set down his rifle and started to adjust the darned shorts once more, an eight-point buck stepped into the opening we were watching. The deer caught the motion, whirled, and disappeared.

Comfort then is one very important aspect of sitting. The immediate surroundings, of course, also are a vital consideration. Stand sitters can be placed in two categories: those who will stay put on the same stand for several hours and those who hunt by a combination of sitting for a half hour, then prowling for a half hour. Comfort and advantages of the selected spot obviously are of greatest importance to the long-term sitter.

Some of the "must" attributes of a long-term stand are as follows.

Be certain the sun, rising or setting, will be behind you, in the deer's eyes, not yours. Make sure the spot where you place your backside — if you're sitting — doesn't have roots, small rocks, or small sticks that will keep you fidgeting. Be sure your sitting spot is dry. If wet, carry something to sit on, such as a square of tarp or dark-dyed sheepskin. Try to arrange your position so your legs aren't straight out. You probably can't keep them that way for hours on end. Does a stub of dead limb poke into your back? Will a small branch scrape against your hat or cap? If so, change your stance or get rid of the protruding branch.

If you have a backrest against a tree trunk, make sure it's comfortable. If you sit on a log, be sure it's big enough so you don't keep twisting and adjusting for comfort. Make certain that dry leaves and especially twigs that may snap are not under your boots, and that you are able — sitting or standing — to plant your feet comfortably. When standing, try to have a limb or stump at proper height for a gun rest, mostly to avoid tiring from holding your rifle. A rest when sitting is fine, but at least sit so one knee can help as a rest for your elbow when shooting.

A lesson I learned long ago is to definitely try to have a rifle rest if your shot is likely to be over 100 yards. In addition, arrange and test the gun position the moment you take the stand, so you're sure the rest is on the level you'll need. Shots presented under 100 yards don't necessarily require a rest. Another lesson I learned the hard way years ago is *never* to have a limb or stub or any other interfering object between the extreme left and extreme right angles at which you may get a shot. I made this a rule when I spooked as fine a whitetail as I've ever seen by whacking the rifle barrel against a limb while trying to get it into position.

In addition to having a clear field to swing your gun barrel, plan carefully as to how much area you intend to watch. Numerous stand hunters attempt to watch too wide an area, especially for whitetails in woodland situations. Mule deer, usually found in more open terrain, seldom present this problem. Trying to watch too wide an area invariably tempts a hunter into looking way over to the left and way over to the right. This results in constant neck craning and movement of the upper body. Sitting still should mean just that — and in the long run will always produce the highest success.

Of course, no one is capable of sitting absolutely immobile for hours. Some movements certainly are permissible. But now we get into a new facet of the sitting art. All movements should be *in slow motion*. On my ranch I have had a wonderful opportunity for many years to observe deer and to experiment with what they see, hear, smell, and to discover what of the messages their senses bring them disturbs them most. I found that quick motions and the sight of a human face at close range are the real spookers.

Therefore, if a fly crawls on your nose, lift a hand ever so slowly to brush it away. Remember to bring the hand down the same way. If you want to sweep your glance across the entire field of vision of your stand, turn your head in slow motion, and then return to straight-ahead vision. Keep your face shadowed whenever possible, and at the very least hold your head away from the edge of your cover. You'll be surprised how much movement will go unseen, or tolerated, by deer if it is extremely slow.

Slight noises behind or to one side of a stand sitter often tempt him into giving away his position. If you hear something, sit absolutely immobile until you can identify what it is.

As for wind direction, obviously it's best if you have the breeze in your face. If you can't arrange that, sit so it blows across you from a front or side angle. That unavoidably will spoil one opposite angle.

The kinds of places to select for stands are innumerable, and a certain type is not necessarily better than others. In fact, both whitetail and mule deer hunters overlook excellent stands because many of them think solely in terms of finding a place to hide among trees or rocks. Wearing tan camo, I once sat down in the edge of a patch of tall, pale, dead grass out away from a woodland edge and had five different whitetails in range within 2 hours. In mule deer country I have often sat among low brush right in the open on a ridge side and watched mule deer moving along a valley.

Ingenious stands of that sort sometimes have advantages over hideaways. Deer aren't inclined to look them over so carefully because they don't appear to be hiding places for a predator. In rocky country, a big boulder may make a good spot, especially if it's one you can lie flat on or simply sit on and become part of the boulder-strewn scene. Wherever you sit, a background of some sort is vitally important. It doesn't always have to be tight against your back, but it should keep you from being silhouetted against the sky.

In mountains or hills, a morning stand high up on the side or near the top of a ridge is a good choice. Deer may be feeding in the valleys or along ridge sides. Thermal currents rise in the morning, keeping your scent from deer below you. Many deer, mule deer in particular, move up at midmorning to bed down, thus sending them to you. Late in the day, thermals descend, and a valley stand on any still day will be best at this time. A close-in backdrop is more important in a valley or in flat country, where you're on a level with the deer. It's not as important, nor is surrounding cover, when you take a stand high on a slope. Deer don't scan upslope as much as straight ahead.

Add up all the factors and you'll find that sitting for deer is truly an exacting art, but one that almost ensures success for the hunter who practices it. "Stand hunting," an old master of it once told me, "is often downgraded as a deer hunting method by the still-hunters because, they say, you don't do anything but sit and wait. They don't realize that 'not doing anything' is a most difficult thing to do."

Hunting by this statistical method will point you to abundant whitetails, and to places where the best antlers come from.

If you will settle for a so-so buck chiefly for the venison, select an area of abundant deer. The author tagged this one in such a place.

CHAPTER 21
COMPUTERIZE YOUR DEER HUNT

Using the "computerized" system is advantageous for mule deer, too. This Utah buck was taken from a pre-selected hunt unit known for a good supply of adult bucks.

It has been my good fortune over many years to hunt deer in numerous states, from Maine to Texas, Michigan to Montana, and down the Rockies clear to Mexico. This has meant planning dozens of hunting trips. I became convinced a long time ago, from experiences of my own and from meeting hundreds of other deer hunters off on trips outside their home states, or to portions of their home states new to them, that most poor hunts are born from inept planning.

Year by year, that conviction is strengthened by contact with other deer hunters. After having written scores of deer hunting articles for various magazines, and dealt with the subject in several books, I receive annually scads of letters and phone calls from readers asking where they might find a good deer hunt. Most seem to be thinking chiefly about what guide to hire, or where a hunt is available at a price they can afford, without much regard at all for *where* and *what kind*.

Granted, money is a consideration. And so is a qualified guide, if one wishes a guided hunt. But it strikes me this somewhat desperation planning has it all backward. The hunter starts with no focus whatever. If hunters would go about it mathematically, gathering abundantly available statistics and fitting them to the type of hunt desired, results invariably would be 100 percent improved.

Certainly there is much to deer hunting in addition to bringing home a deer. But I suspect that those who say they really don't care whether or not they succeed aren't being entirely honest. At the very least, a hunter who sets out on a deer hunting trip hopes to have opportunities for shots, hopes to *see* a satisfactory number of deer, of the variety, size, and sex he is after. There are ways you can substantially help to assure that this will happen.

Cost of a hunt, within reason, and whether or not to use a guide and which one, should all be decisions made last, not first. As an example, one of a group of four hunters from New York State phoned me prior to last season and asked what I'd suggest about a hunt in Texas, where I live. Texas has lots of deer but is a tough state in which to set up a hunt because there is so little public land.

I described one package hunt with which I was familiar. Beautiful country, excellent lodging and food, transport and guide, shots guaranteed or no pay. I explained that I could not recommend cheap hunts, such as day hunting, but could point them to it if that was what they wanted. It seemed to me if one was going to travel from New York to Texas it was not good business to try to cut too many corners.

Upshot was that the party split. Two took the package I had described and had a wonderful hunt, as they later wrote me. Both killed big bucks, and each also collected a doe. The other two were dropped off at a day-hunt place, paid $10 per day for hunting privilege, and found that the landowner had packed his place. They had difficulties with lodging and food, bagged one forkhorn, spent an exasperating and far from pleasant several days.

In planning any deer hunt, the first thing to decide is what sort of deer you want. The species choice is, of course, obvious — whitetail or mule deer. But then an astute hunter should bone up on subspecies, so he knows, for example, that some whitetails are much larger than others, and doesn't expect a mule deer of Rocky Mountain mule deer size if he is going to hunt where only the slightly smaller desert mule deer live. He should also be crafty about checking certain areas that have both whitetail and mule deer. Just maybe he can get a license in a two-deer area where he can try for one of each, which makes an interesting hunt, indeed.

Next, you need to decide how choosy you will be. Will you be strictly trophy hunting? If so, you need to define, for your purposes, what "trophy" means to you. If it means a buck that might make the record book, then a careful study of the North American Big Game Awards Program records is invaluable. The record book, prepared by The Boone and Crockett Club and the National Rifle Association, is available from NRA. Certain areas of the continent have been producing trophy deer for years, and certain ones have produced none, or few. Pay particular attention to areas, such as counties or sectors of a state, that have consistently put records into the book over the past 10 or 15 years.

Classic, dramatic examples that occur to me of what a study of the book will show you are tied up in statistics for blacktail deer of the Pacific coast, and the Coues deer of the Southwest. California has put about 45 percent of the total of blacktail heads into the book, most of them from a very few northern counties. Coues deer records from Arizona simply overwhelm those from New Mexico. For record-book hunters, these would seem to be the logical choices for hunting these deer.

But perhaps "trophy" in your view means just a darned big rack, maybe by luck one for the book but at least a bragging one for the wall. This of course broadens the picture considerably. And here you get down to asking questions from state game departments. Specific questions. Every state knows where its largest-racked deer come from. Maine, for example, has very few heads in the book, but nonetheless turns up some excellent racks, with the best chances probably in Aroostock and Washington Counties. You can find out from any state this valuable statistic — where in general the largest heads originate.

Or will you settle for just any buck — or for that matter any deer? If so, the question now gets down to success percentages and regional kill statistics. Every state keeps tabs on its deer kill and number of deer hunters. The comparison shows at a glance the success level, whether it runs, say one hunter in seven, one out of four, two out of three. Selecting from several states, it is obvious that the higher the average hunter success, the better your odds, and the more deer you are likely to see.

Now narrow it down, to counties, or hunt units in those states that use a unit system. That information is also on tap. You'll discover that most counties or hunt units show a fairly consistent kill and success level season after season. Where a given number of permits is issued for a certain unit, and the kill accounts for a high percentage of them, this is bound to be a place where there are a good many deer, and where chances of a kill are excellent. Keep in mind that this doesn't have anything to do with trophies. These are simply deer and hunter statistics.

Some states — Pennsylvania is one — annually publish a harvest map. The Pennsylvania map shows, by counties, the kill of antlered and antlerless deer. Certainly a high-kill county with a large number of bucks taken tells you this must be a good location. What it doesn't tell you is how many hunters were competing. So, try to get a success percentage figure for the county, or hunt unit. Many states have such figures.

As you study statistics you've gathered, relate them to how you like to hunt. Maybe you are one of those who wants to be far back in the wilderness and hunt in a totally uncrowded area. Look then for counties or units of large area that have a comparatively low kill, and even a modest success percentage. These suggest no crowding, plenty of room to roam, and just maybe a chance at a big deer. The moderate-sized herd is probably not as hard pressured as elsewhere and thus some of the bucks live longer.

Conversely, some hunters like plenty of other hunters around to keep deer moving. Management statistics showing a high kill, of both sexes, unquestionably means a lot of deer, and a lot of hunters, particularly if the area is of nominal size. If the success percentage here is only so-so, it's a sure bet a lot of hunters are after a lot of deer. Look also very carefully at the antlerless kills and number of antlerless permits. If you just want a deer, regardless of sex, the areas with numerous antlerless permits invariably mean too many deer for the range, management attempts to cut down the herd, and thus good hunting. However, in these areas there are not likely to be very many large-antlered bucks. They have been pared down closely for some time.

A most revealing statistic, and one available from a number of states, is the kill per square mile in a given area. A New Hampshire friend of mine told me a few years ago that he watches these closely in his home state. That state has kept figures for townships, which is cutting it mighty fine, and in these right down to kill per square mile. As an example, several years ago in Coos County, Dummer township, there was a kill of 232 deer, which amounted to 4.81 per square mile. A square mile is a section of land — 640 acres. If the kill over the entire township amounted to almost five deer per section, you can bet there were plenty of deer to choose from.

Washington state also has kept such statistics. A good example of what they can show you is taken from figures I gathered a few seasons ago on several counties there. Island Co., for example, had a kill that year of 1,130 deer. The area of the county is 206 square miles. Thus the harvest was about 5.48 deer per square mile. You can gather from such figures that there must be an overpopulation of deer. This is an open invitation to success, if your hunt plans call for this kind of hunt. You can just about bet that:

A — chances will be good.
B — hunting will probably be fairly crowded to extremely crowded.
C — chances of a trophy deer will be slim because such a heavy kill means mostly young, and antlerless, deer.

I must interject here that it may seem strange to some readers to be setting store for a coming season by what occurred during the last, or last several. Fact is, deer management today is a rather exact science. There may be perplexing and unanswered questions about why a deer herd slowly declines, or builds up. But deer experts know pretty well how to set quotas, or from seasonal surveys set seasons to achieve roughly the kill needed so as not to hasten a decline or to allow too swift a buildup.

Therefore, deer populations and harvests seldom fluctuate drastically, as harvests and populations of short-lived game birds may. I have made comparisons, for example, of state deer kills, and county kills, for as long a period as 10 years in selected states, and have discovered a surprising similarity and consistency. It is interesting that deer biologists are able to recommend, in quota instances, a given number of hundreds of permits for a certain unit, and predict within astonishingly narrow and accurate margins what the actual kill will be. They do it by projecting success percentages on that area from past seasons.

Thus you can be reasonably certain that past recent statistics actually forecast quite accurately what can be expected in at least the near future. There may be some exceptions, but even these a sharp hunter can use advantageously. For instance, let's say a high antlerless quota is set for Unit 1 in a certain state, and the harvest shows that the kill was attained. You are applying for a license for the coming season, and note that as high an antlerless quota is offered. You know that the herd buildup has not been stopped, and that the same situation will exist as last season. Conversely, if you look at that high quota for the foregoing year and see a very low quota upcoming, you read from this that maybe you should steer shy of this area if you want any deer. Probably the herd has been cut way down, and though the area may be a perennial trouble spot of overpopulation, it may not be much overpopulated again for several years.

Now, of course, few hunters will be able any given season to go just anywhere they might wish. So, before you plan *where*, settle on what sort of hunt you hope to experience. Then begin to estimate how far away you'll be able to travel to get it — which will be related both to the time and the money you can invest. When you've made a circle on the map indicating a possible region for hunting, you begin to know which states or provinces you'll need information from. Keep it reasonable. Otherwise you'll have so many statistics you'll confuse yourself.

Be sure you don't overlook portions of your home state with which you are not acquainted. As an illustration: some years ago when I lived in northern Michigan, I thought I had terrific deer hunting practically on my doorstep. But a cousin of mine from southern Michigan used to stop each season on his way north, only he went far past where I lived, to a remote part of the Upper Peninsula. And when he came back, he invariably stopped, and he always had a deer, a buster buck. It took several years for it to sink in on me, after I'd gathered some figures from the state, that I was hunting at home in a rather crowded area with modest success potential and few big bucks, whereas the region my cousin had found was uncrowded, had fewer deer but a higher success for those who persevered, and offered much better chances at trophy bucks.

For instance, there may be a piece of farm country in your state that doesn't seem like much for deer. But it also may be a sleeper. Perhaps a study of what goes on there will show you awesomely fat, big, and very crafty deer, not many hunters, and a most intriguing variety of hunting. Some astonishing deer come out of the farm country of states like Illinois, Nebraska, Minnesota, and South Dakota every season. A county by county study of any area will help you establish the locations of such appealing pockets.

When you get down to figuring costs and what you can afford, the most economical hunt is not necessarily the best choice, as I said earlier. To be sure, if you are intimately acquainted with a piece of deer country, can go and camp on it and keep every cost low, then you can enjoy a good experience at a low price. But if that is the case, you don't need statistical planning. However, as everyone knows, nowadays hunting competition is keen, and all costs are up. Although it is not entirely true that the more you spend, the better your chances of success, it is true that you cannot buy quality, especially on a range unfamiliar to you, at any bargain price.

I have a group of friends who go after mule deer in west Texas each season. They pay $100 per gun for a part of a big ranch they lease for a week. In Texas mule deer country, which is extremely limited, that is cheap. About one hundred miles from where they hunt, the lowest rate one could possibly get is $500, and some ranches charge much more. Competition has pushed prices up. A check of state surveys of the mule deer herd year after year will show, however, that the fellows who pay only $100 are paying the really high price — because the deer count is extremely low where they hunt, and extremely high in the prime areas where the seemingly high prices occur.

Those who hunt the quality range see sometimes as many as 100 or more deer a day, often as many as 20 shootable bucks a day. In my estimation, the value is not that the hunting is easy on the quality range as against tough on the marginal range. It's simply that seeing game hour after hour is a dramatic experience, and there's always the feeling that you should hold out for a bigger buck. The excitement and enjoyment are at a constant high level. Conversely, on the poor range those $100 hunters some seasons see only three or four deer all told, are lucky to bag one or two among 10 hunters. The onus is on them to shoot the first buck sighted. I'd rather make one good hunt than two or three exasperating ones. Herd surveys can easily prove where the money values lie!

Another statistic traveling deer hunters would be well advised to note is the average success percentage among guided hunters, as compared to those going it on their own. Almost without fail, the hunters who hire guides or book a guided or package hunt show a much higher success ratio than those who do not. Interestingly, non-resident hunters in states where many are guided, or in the past in some states where guides were required for non-residents, are always well ahead of resident hunters in success percentage.

Of course, there are numerous regions where there are no guides. Guided hunts are as a rule more common for mule deer than for whitetails. There are logical reasons why guided hunters are consistently more successful. Foremost in importance, I presume, is the fact that a guide makes his living by his endeavors. If he builds a poor reputation for success, it follows him. Thus, he makes it a point to know the best areas, and he works hard to get deer for his hunters.

The guided hunt certainly costs more, but it gets results. I've watched guides in Wyoming work with awesome determination to run a big-headed mule deer out of a canyon in front of a hunter. The hunter, new to such territory, might not realize the places the deer will hide, nor on his own be pushed with such stubborn effort toward success. It's as if a guide were saying, "My reputation is at stake here, and you'll get a good deer if I have to walk you into the ground!" The extra cost is well worth it when you look at statistics that show (as I have seen some) resident, unguided hunters with success of around 40 percent and guided non-residents with 90 percent.

I have a friend who is a guide in Texas for whitetails. He owns about 30,000 acres and leases another 10,000. He books an average of around 200 hunters each season, figures his herd can support that large a kill, and for some seasons now he has had within a hair of a 100 percent kill for his hunters. Many of them, like many hunters anywhere, are on a snug schedule. Time also is money. Thus it is comforting to know when you book a hunt that you are going to see plenty of deer, be offered ample opportunities for shots, and have an excellent chance of taking a good buck. In strange territory, especially, all this is comforting, even at added expense.

Deer hunters sometimes also overlook some very common, easily acquired figures that can help with planning. If you are going to a distant state with which you are unfamiliar, make it a point to look up how large it is in square miles, what the population is, where the majority of the people live (in a few large urban centers or scattered more generally). Find out from the state how many deer hunters participate each season on the average, and how many are nonresident.

Believe it or not, there are still a few states left, in the plains and the mountains particularly, that have moderate human population, a lot of wide-open areas, and only modest hunting pressure on their deer. A few of these are states with low advertising budgets. They don't sing their own praises very loudly, and occasionally have some well-kept secrets worth prying into. Hunting permission on privately-owned lands is usually easier to come by in such places.

Further, check with the state of your choice as to public lands. How much acreage is in National Forests, State Forests if any, State Public Hunting Areas, etc.? In any state with a high number of deer hunters, the smaller the public-land acreage, the more crowded, and the less the success as a rule. Yet in huge National Forests, much of the acreage may be inaccessible except via horseback or four-wheel-drive, and even the latter is seeing numerous restrictions nowadays. A hunter with only a short time to spend, and who is a stranger to the region, does not have much latitude on a million-acre forest if only some fringes are easily accessible to him.

Let me suggest one more check to be made, always as late as possible in your planning. As we all know, a number of states nowadays hunt on a quota system, with only a specified number of permits for various areas available, and application required rather early. Across the northern states, severe winters occasionally decimate deer herds. In southern regions a drought or other debacle may have similar effects. Thus if you plan to hunt some distance from your home state, keep informed about the weather and condition of the deer during the winter and summer prior to the season. A heavy die-off may make a switch in plans from one region to another advisable, assuming there is time for a change.

If you start gathering facts on which to base hunt plans, you will be surprised at what a vast amount of information is available for the asking. But one caution — game department people are busy, and too commonly harassed by all sorts of unbelievably inane crackpot querries. Don't class yourself among these. Be specific, and brief. Ask, for example, for kill statistics for the past season, or several. List what you want to know: buck kill, doe kill, for instance, kills by counties, or maybe only specified counties that sound good to you, success percentage for the state, for counties specified if available, and so on. So-called "fishing expedition" requests won't get much for you. Know what you want and ask precisely for it.

Such an approach to hunt planning can change your deer hunting entirely, making it more successful, and more interesting. It's really a matter of first deciding what kind of hunt you want, and then mathematically tracking it down.

Mule deer in thin or low cover are not as spooky as whitetails. Often it's possible, as here, to get within range.

This buck had no cover at all, was bedded beside the low bush showing in photo. Open country mule deer often apparently are covninced they're hidden when they're not.

CHAPTER 22

THIN COVER MULE DEER

This buck was jumped from a gully not seen in photo, by hunter walking up it. Camera hunter walking beside the deep cut demonstrates how two hunters can work successfully together in gully-slashed plains areas.

Each deer season hundreds of whitetail hunters from the eastern two-thirds of the nation go west after their first mule deer, and hundreds of Westerners also make their first mule deer hunt. All these inexperienced hunters, and a great many also from both parts of the country who are already muley hunters, think of all deer as creatures clinging to dense cover. This is particularly true of those who've always hunted whitetails, but numerous Westerners also equate mule deer to timber. Some muleys certainly do live in and near forests. The fact is, however, that the mule deer hunter who shuns the heavy timber and sticks to *thin* cover over the long haul comes out way ahead.

Unlike the whitetail, which certainly is an animal of heavy cover and its edges, the mule deer is fundamentally not a "woods" animal at all, regardless of ingrained hunter concepts. To be sure, mule deer are found in mountain forests. But of all their vast Western range, the forests are the least important and harbor the fewest animals. It is true that now and then an extra-large trophy buck is discovered far back in conifers near some remote, small mountain meadow. But for every one so located there are a hundred out on the sparsely covered slopes.

In the higher mountain country, most Rocky Mountain mule deer spend summers above or at the edge of timberline. When they make a vertical downward migration in fall as heavy snows come to the alpine areas, they wind up in foothills where sage, scattered juniper, varied brush, and dwarf oaks are the habitat. You hear a lot about these deer, but probably the most typical of prime mule deer habitats are year-round areas in mountain foothills where juniper and sage merge higher up with scattered piñon, other conifers, and aspen. There are also many areas — parts of eastern Wyoming, for example — where mule deer are abundant, and yet, except for a very few ancient cottonwoods along creek courses, there's not a sizable tree for 100 miles.

Whether the thin cover produces a preponderance of record heads is beside the point. I'm writing here of consistent *success*. For over twenty years I have made at least one hunt each fall for the desert mule deer subspecies, which ranges from southwestern Texas across southern New Mexico and Arizona. This terrain, with some low brush in draws and on flats, Spanish bayonet speckling the slopes, and dabs of juniper here and there, with rocky slopes and countless hidden canyons, is some of the best mule deer country on the continent. The area also provides a great education for any mule deer hunter because it illustrates so well what thin cover mule deer range is and where you should look for deer in such country.

All you do, once out of this southwestern desert-mountain terrain, is transpose habitat ingredients. Sagebrush foothills farther north, with small copses perhaps of aspen, here and there a few pines, brushy draws, willow-bordered creek bottoms, the ever-present junipers of one species or another, all invariably sustain abundant mule deer populations, and these places are where success comes easiest to the hunter. The reason is simple: he can see far without heavy timber obstructing the view.

An excellent illustration of the importance of this simple concept as related to success occurred one fall when I made two mule deer hunts, one in forest country in Colorado, one in the Big Bend region of western Texas. There was ample deer sign where we hunted in both places. On the Colorado hunt, however, the only time deer were easily spotted was very early and very late along the edges of timber-fringed mountain meadows. In the timber during the day I heard and glimpsed many muleys, but I had no chances for shots. I finally bagged a modest-sized buck, the only one at which I really had a fair chance. In the open mountains of the Big Bend I quite literally took my pick. I never saw less than a dozen good-size bucks a day in shootable situations.

I once made a list of favorite types of mule deer cover that I've hunted successfully. They all added up to thin or almost nonexistent cover. Remember that deer utilize what is available in their home bailiwicks. The mule deer born to the timber naturally moves into it to bed down, where it is difficult to see or find. The one raised on an open slope where only a few scattered bushes break up the scenery commonly beds down in the shade of one of those. If a slope is totally bereft of cover, the deer moves up shortly after dawn and beds down in a shady pocket somewhere along a rimrock. There's nowhere else.

On numerous occasions, in wide-open mule deer country, I've watched deer walk across a slope, drop over the lip of a small draw, and disappear. Many such draws I'm visualizing are not over a few feet deep, but they run from the flat at the bottom of the slope on up to the top of the ridge. Invariably these are wider and shallower near the flat at the base of the ridge and narrower at the top. Brush and rocks often are present in them. Scores of mule deer lie down in these. As a rule the deer will be part way up the slope. However, one may be anywhere along such a small, inconsequential draw in open or thin-cover terrain.

The reason most hunters don't bag mule deer on slopes where only a few widely scattered bushes grow, or in similar places, is that *they don't look there.* They're thinking in terms of a great mass of cover in which deer may hide. Sure, deer may be in such places. But they can be almost *anywhere* in such cover, whereas in the thin areas there are only so many places where a deer can successfully hide. Again, don't overlook those few scattered bushes or grass clumps on a ridgeside. Don't sweep a glass over that single rock that casts a bit of shade high on an open slope.

I've picked up in a binocular scores of mule deer bedded in such places. It's a tactic that requires patience. But you can sit on a ridge with binoculars in hand, comb every single bush and every rock, and sometimes thrill yourself by spotting half a dozen mule deer all within rifle range that you can barely believe are there. They'll stay lying right there, too, unless crowded. If you're a tyro and have been a whitetail hunter, you should not discount these possibilities on the most-open slopes in sight.

One of my great memories of mule deer hunting is of watching through binoculars ten big ten-pointers scattered out along a ridge, feeding in early morning. Not one bush or rock big enough to hide a deer was in sight. After a while they drifted upward and faded from sight into the jumble of a seemingly barren rimrock. Most hunters, passing in a vehicle or afoot, would not have given this region a cursory glance. How could it be deer country without much cover?

Certainly there are parts of mule deer range where no such thin-cover expanses are present. If I were planning a hunt, however, especially if time were limited, I'd set it up in meager-cover country. Almost all foothills are good bets. Look for sage, juniper, and rocky rims. Open, rather arid terrain, backed up against steep cliffs where jumbled rocks are present and gnarled and scattered junipers offer shade, is perfect. The lower country all along the eastern slope of the Rockies, and again on the western slope, contains massive expanses that are perfectly tailored.

In the treeless foothills, you'll often see rolling terrain, with stark shale upthrusts here and there and land cut by deep coulees. Often this is ranch country, where irrigated fields of alfalfa are present. Some of the best mule deer hunting in the U.S. is present in such places. The deer bed down on the rough shale hills or in the deep coulees and washes. This type of region is by passed as poor deer range by many hunters.

Eastern Washington and Oregon have a lot of thin-cover mule deer range. So do Nevada and portions of eastern California. Eastern New

Mexico and the Texas panhandle, where the big and ancient river canyons gouge the land, are perfect. I've already mentioned the Southwestern desert mule deer range, which offers delightful hunting with high success percentages. The rugged region of redrock cliffs and scattered vegetation in eastern Utah also is an excellent bet.

You must be sure that in your search for the right terrain you don't hunt the early season on what is strictly winter mule deer range. In certain places there are few mule deer in summer, but a heavy downward migration from high country after fall storms does materialize. Those migrations end on what is ancestral winter range. There may be much old sign, that is, droppings from the previous winter, browse-eating evidence also from that time, weathered antlers, etc. Such heavy vertical seasonal migrations are usually well known to local hunters and almost certainly to game-department biologists.

In planning a hunt, it is not difficult to avoid settling on an area definitely known as winter range. Vast numbers of mule deer throughout their range are not migratory; they live on the same range year round. Game department personnel can advise you. Furthermore, if you avoid the regions where the backdrop is exceptionally high country, usually you are on safe ground. Much of eastern Montana and Wyoming serve as classic examples. Here along the stream courses, and in lightly timbered regions far removed from the big mountains, mule deer thrive and have no high country from which to move down to winter range.

Where there are vehicle trails along valleys, some hunters may prefer cruising, then pausing often to glass. If you use a horse, going slowly is mandatory. It is too often presumed that horses don't spook mule deer. Don't you believe it! Even in timber the deer will move out when they hear horses coming. In open country they will run more quickly from the sound of horses on shale than they will from a vehicle moving along a trail.

Glassing, then stalking is what fills tags in thin-cover terrain. I prefer to find sign in an area offering little cover. In such habitats there are fewer logical places for deer to be.

Remember, glassing is an all-day proposition in such thin-cover country. Early and late, deer will be active and extremely visible. Keep in mind that thermals rise as the sun warms the slopes and settle late in the day when dusk cools the country. In some areas this knowledge will dictate where you should sit to do your glassing.

Regardless, I like to study open slopes when walking, or riding, from below during the middle of the day. A mule deer bedded by a single rock or bush, I've found, seldom will spook when looked at from below unless you crowd it. It assumes it is unseen. But if you're above, the deer gets nervous. Once you spot one from below while you're in a "thin" cover, you should keep right on going, circle, and climb over a ridgetop or do whatever else is necessary to stealthily get yourself within range. The fact that deer around thin cover are so often where you'd seen them earlier vastly enhances your numerical chances of hunting success.

Of course plans don't always work out the way you'd like them to. Rimrocks easily hide mule deer . . . so do old junipers scattered along the base of a cliff or rim . . . so do deep washes where they lie up in cool headers, often near a seep. You must climb up to the rims and work along them quietly and diligently. Sometimes a deft hunter can take a buck in its bed up there. More often he'll get short-range "jump shooting." Hunting the deep erosions is a different proposition. To do it properly requires two people, one walking the bottom, the other up on the top keeping a short distance ahead of his companion.

Many mule deer hunters just can't bring themselves to believe their quarry lives in the kinds of places I have described. Once you start hunting such terrain, however, you'll be surprised at what you'll discover. Scouting thin cover is the easiest and by far the most successful approach to mule deer hunting. It's more enjoyable also because you see so many deer.

When deer are feeding they must move around, and go from forage to resting place. Such movements are of utmost importance to hunter success.

Whenever deer move they leave tracks. Always check spots of bare ground in your hunting area for this important sign.

CHAPTER 23

WHITETAILS ON THE MOVE

Deer move to water as a rule every day, and in warm weather more often. Watching a watering place, especially where water is not abundant, may bring you success.

Four of us were camped in the thornbrush and cactus near the Texas-Mexico border, a region that has produced numerous record and trophy whitetail racks. This was our annual hunt for "a big one." Weather had been scorching hot for three days, and we still hadn't seen so much as a fawn.

We were sleeping without covers on cots this third breezeless night when, about 3 A.M., a swirl of wind suddenly rattled the old camphouse. Everyone awoke. For few minutes the wind was stiff and cool. Then it was chilly. We stumbled around gathering covers.

"That's a small front moving through," someone said.

A few minutes later someone else got up and squirted a flashlight beam at the thermometer fastened to the wall of the old shack.

"Dropped 10 degrees," he said. "We'd better be out there before daylight. Deer are going to be traveling."

At daylight we were out in the brush, cruising around. As predicted, so were the deer. The sky was overcast; there was a gentle breeze from the northwest. Although the temperature had changed by only that sudden 10-degree drop, deer seemed to pop out of the ground and *were* traveling. Two big ones went onto the hanging pole that morning. The other two hunters in our party turned down deer that didn't quite measure up.

That experience was one of the most memorable examples I can recall of how intimate knowledge of the where, when, and, especially, *why* of whitetail movements can point you toward success. We all knew that after a few still, blistering days in this desert country, even a small temperature drop and an overcast sky would trigger deer travel. Farther north, say in New England, a more drastic change might be needed to produce as much movement as we saw, which illustrates that the subject of whitetail travel is indeed a complicated one.

It is, however, the chief basis upon which the plans, and successes, of the majority of whitetail hunters annually hinge. Harvest studies in numerous places have shown that as many as 90 percent of whitetails bagged availed themselves to hunters because they were moving around and exposing themselves. Only a small percentage are shot in their beds or taken when jumped from their hiding and resting places. To be consistently successful, a whitetail hunter needs to amass as much travel information as he possibly can.

Whitetails are not wide-ranging travelers. Many live out their lives within a square mile or less. But each deer, going about the business of living and of trying to find daily comfort and safety, sets up travel routines. These change to some extent with the seasons. Hunters are interested, of course, only in those movements, and the reasons for them, that occur during deer season. In states where the season is brief, the whys and wherefores of whitetail travels are somewhat simplified. In states with long seasons, routines commonly change at least slightly several times during the season.

The basic reasons for whitetail movements are simple enough. They travel from resting places to feeding places, then move on to water, and finally head back to resting locations. (They also travel during the rut, and they move when disturbed by hunter pressure; however, these are specialized movements outside the scope of what we're discussing here.) What complicates the study of the normal daily travel routines is that numerous natural influences, which whimsically can change from day to day, incessantly cause the animals to alter what should be routine movements.

Practically all of these whimsical movements are in some way related to weather. And it may not be weather of the moment. Consider weather and its long-range influence on forage. In my area, acorns are a staple fall food. When spring and summer weather is such that our abundant and varied oaks produce a bumper crop, deer travel for feeding purposes diminishes. They don't have to move far to fill up. The astute hunter, realizing this, doesn't expect to see so much helter-skelter deer activity, but he does base his hunting on the oaks. Conversely, when the acorns fail, we get easier hunting because the deer have to work harder. They move around more, and for longer periods, which means they are more vulnerable. The drawback is that they're seldom in as good physical condition as deer taken in good acorn years.

Throughout the vast and highly varied range of the whitetail, a hunter must concentrate on what influences deer movement in his region. Using acorn abundance as a deer guide would be useless on many ranges. Deer eat dozens of different plants and twigs. I've watched deer in the Great Lakes region wandering aimlessly among maples and poplars, nipping a reachable twig here, another there. In such a situation, there is no one forage that attracts whitetails from a wide area and concentrates them in a small area. On the other hand, on any evening during the season in the Texas Hill Country, where winter oat patches are numerous, you can count from a dozen to fifty or more deer on almost every field. They come out of surrounding cover, move around little, fill up in a hurry, and move back into protective cover.

Each hunter, therefore, must study what forage occurs where he hunts.

What deer are eating, and where, is especially important because the bulk of whitetail travel, and the hours that it occurs, are involved with keeping a full stomach. We all know that whitetails are normally most active early and late in the day. But that's not quite all of it. Whitetails are cud chewers. They fill up, or partially so, then retire to chew the cud. They eat, when some weather influence doesn't upset the pattern, every 4 to 6 hours.

Once you get past the matter of normal feeding and activity periods, the plot thickens. Temperature gremlins, for one, begin to upset your neat theories. Numerous researchers have concluded that, in general, whitetails are most active and contented in what might be termed average good weather. That means weather that is not extreme — no hard winds, rains, low skies, heat waves, or blizzards. Researchers have also concluded that whitetail activity and feeling of well-being lessens as temperature creeps above what would be considered normal for the given time of year. This seems to be true throughout whitetail range.

Thus, travel diminishes as temperatures increase, and when temperatures are well above normal, daytime travel may cease entirely. When the temperature drops, whitetails will resume their travels.

Keep in mind that this temperature-movement ratio is comparative; it's related to where you hunt.

Normal or below-normal temperature is conducive to normal deer routines. But there is a limit; when the temperature plummets and a severe front is coming, there will be frenzied activity just before the front hits. Then things shut down completely. This phenomenon is more pronounced in the Midsouth and South. Whitetails in the Southwest simply disappear during an unusual snowstorm. In northern Michigan a storm that mild has little effect except for some revved-up activity before and after. Activity during the clearing period following a hard storm anywhere is invariably exaggerated. This is a prime whitetail hunting time.

Extremes of temperature either way tend to upset whitetail travel routines. Some years ago in Michigan I noticed that when the temperature was unusually low for a couple of days, but the days were sunny, morning deer activity didn't seem drastically affected. After a cold night deer appeared to be eager to move out into the sun. Late afternoon saw less activity, however, as shadows and bitter cold drew down.

When I moved to Texas, I discovered an identical reaction at the opposite end of the temperature scale. On hot days deer movement was fairly good very early, at first shooting light. The deer apparently took advantage of the coolest time of day to move about. Late in the afternoon, even though the temperature had dropped some, it was still too hot. The deer waited until sundown to start moving.

Does barometric pressure influence whitetail movement? Some hunters are convinced it does. Certain studies tend to prove it does, but I suspect some of them started out to prove that. Barometric-pressure studies have been done on numerous species of wildlife. My own observations, and those of friends who have kept track of deer activity in relation to the barometer, seem to show a correlation.

A rancher friend who takes fee hunters recently told me, "For ten deer seasons I kept track of the daily kill and the barometer reading. I didn't count kills of deer in bedding areas, but only those bagged when they were moving. Generally high kill numbers occurred on high-barometer days."

But then he qualified his statement. "Maybe this means whitetails are more active on a high barometer. Maybe it means that a high barometer simply indicates a weather pattern that causes the activity."

Indeed, so complicated are the influences that, studies notwith-standing, mysteries will remain. Nevertheless, if a hunter sets up a basic plan, then uses common sense to figure out why the rules suddenly don't work, he will come out pretty well in guessing deer activity. For example, though deer don't commonly move about in overcast, humid days, if such days have been preceded by blistering temperatures, the relative coolness afforded by cloud cover can often induce whitetail movement.

Rain also exerts a profound influence on whitetail movements. Deer will travel during a warm drizzle, but I've never taken a buck in a downpour. Wind is yet another important determinant. Since a stiff wind creates too much background noise, which dampens a deer's aural acuity, deer are very reluctant to move during a steady blow.

The travels of whitetails to and from food, water, and resting areas offer you the best opportunity to fill a tag. Though these movements are complex and depend on a complicated set of interrelated natural factors, they can be plotted with a reasonable degree of accuracy. The more you learn about the traveling habits of deer, the better your chances of bringing home a buck.

Even when there seems to be no breeze, the slightest movement of air from behind you will alert any deer in that direction.

This buck indicates that it has heard some strange sound. Even the rustle of a nylon jacket as you move an arm may be picked up by a buck nearby.

CHAPTER 24
MAKING SENSE OF DEER SENSES

Always move in slow motion. Deer sight is not much better than yours, but *movement* will be detected instantly.

Every beginning deer hunter learns from his mentors and from all he reads that the senses of deer are awesomely keen. But just *how* keen is too commonly overblown. It has been claimed that a deer can see the flick of a hunter's eyelash a mile away, that it hears the grass grow and the sands of time running, that it can pick up scent from a cigarette three ridges over, and so forth. These near-miraculous powers would seem to indicate that deer almost never make mistakes.

It's true that the senses of deer are finely tuned, and are better developed in many ways than the senses of the hunter. Much progress in becoming a truly expert deer hunter is thwarted when a beginning hunter accepts the propaganda that deer senses are honed to the point of infallibility. A careful, realistic rating of the pertinent senses of deer compared to those of the hunter is far more helpful than the exaggerations. Even more important is understanding not just what deer see, hear, and smell, but how they interpret it.

Unquestionably smell is the keenest deer sense. One season I was hunting on my ranch and made a careful, slow-motion stalk through fairly open cedars that brought me to the edge of a rock outcrop possibly 10 feet above a creek. It overlooked a stretch of rather open valley. A whitetail buck, head down and feeding, was approximately 100 yards away. I had outwitted all of its senses for the moment. From the buck's point of view, I might have been visible several times as I moved to this position. If it actually could hear as well as the exaggerators claim, it should have heard me, for I had crackled leaves once and even clinked a rock.

I stood immobile and well-screened and I eased my binoculars up and studied the deer. It raised its head alertly, but it was not disturbed. Suddenly a puff of wind whirled between the ridges and hit me in the face. Then, as air currents so often do in canyon country, it swirled around and touched the back of my neck. The deer didn't even pause to look my way. It threw up its tail and rocketed off into the timber.

A diligent study of horned and antlered game animals and their senses quickly unearths the fact that those living in heavy cover invariably have an extremely well-developed sense of smell. The whitetail is one of these. It needs this sense to be razor sharp because it commonly lives in places where vision is limited and where it may also be vulnerable to a stealthy, silent approach.

Obviously, all three important deer senses are used as scanning devices against danger. Watch the whitetail closely, however. If it first sees something suspicious, it may automatically cock its ears in that direction, but what it tries most urgently to do is get a whiff of what it has seen or heard and thereby differentiate between something dangerous and not dangerous.

If you were to purposely alert a whitetail by some slight motion or sound, the deer wouldn't run immediately. It would peer, cock its ears, and get its nose working. If it scented nothing disturbing, it might go back to feeding again. However, let either or both sight and hearing be alerted, then scent be added, or let the sense of smell be the first brought into focus, and the whitetail is gone.

Interestingly, Rocky Mountain mule deer and their subspecies, except the blacktail, are a bit different. Their sense of smell may be just as acute, but their habitat is far different, being made up of slopes and many open areas. Mule deer are not authentic forest animals, but creatures of open ridges, mountain meadows, low foothill brush, and often sparse stands of trees. Here they are able to see for great distances. Here thermal currents rise as the day warms, then flow downward as the sun lowers. The deer therefore go *up* very often to bed down, where thermals bring them scents rising from below. Oddly, they are not too concerned about what is above, and that is regularly a fatal mistake. They are *looking* more intently than scenting. Blacktails in their dense cover can be compared to whitetails.

There is no comparison between the keenness of the senses of smell in deer and in man. Compared to theirs, ours is ludicrously underdeveloped. However, as reasoning creatures we contrive to thwart our quarry's sense of smell by trying to keep even the slightest air movement in our favor — that means toward us, or at least crossways. But we definitely cannot compete for even footing with deer where scent is concerned.

I'm one who is unwilling to admit, however, that a healthy human's hearing is much less acute than that of deer. Certainly a deer's ears are fashioned so that they funnel in sound waves better than ours. But a deer hunter who practices listening, as well as silence, can come fairly close to matching that sense with his quarry.

I think of an evening when my son Mike, then in his teens, and I made an oh-so-careful prowl up a steep ridge on our ranch. Juniper, oak, and other growth was heavy. Leaves were an obstacle to silence. Tall dead grass in places stood to our knees. We moved in slow motion, searching each step for a flat, stable rock on which to put a boot down. We paused often to look and listen.

The air was utterly still. During one pause we heard a rustling sound. In our area armadillos make rustling sounds in leaves, but that is erratically distinctive. This was too regular. It translated as the sound of a deer walking slowly down the draw before us.

We had been walking up, and the deer had been walking down. It had not heard us, but we had heard it at least fifty paces away. The deer, an eight-point buck whitetail, walked to within five paces of us, then stopped seemingly in astonishment when it finally saw us.

A careful hunter who wears soft clothing that doesn't rustle to impair his hearing and who listens, as one old hand used to tell me, with three ears can compete in the hearing category with deer. Deer certainly can hear fine and far, but so can a hunter who trains himself to do so.

The eyesight of deer is excellent, but it has deficiencies. A deer's depth perception apparently is not as finely developed as ours, and its ability to see colors is limited. There has been much discussion about whether or not deer are totally color blind. Some recent studies indicate that their eyes do contain at least some cells that relay color images. Nevertheless, most hunters who argue that deer see colors plainly confuse color with intensity. Hunter orange, for example, may not be seen as that color but simply as an out-of-place brightness of a shape that doesn't belong in the scene.

In general, the deer hunter who schools himself on how to look for deer, and who does so intently, is able to compete admirably. *Movement* is what deer vision is best at recording. Immobile shapes routinely have little meaning and are difficult for deer to identify, particularly if the human face cannot be distinguished as such.

What causes most hunter errors and perplexity about the senses of deer, and has been examined little in print, is how deer bring all senses to focus on a problem discovered by a single sense. It's this combined usage that so often upsets hunter schemes. Both whitetail and blacktail deer keep scent and hearing keyed up more than sight because of their dense habitat. Rocky Mountain mule deer and their most closely related subspecies rely on sight incessantly, and they use scent and hearing to identify what is seen.

This one-by-one focusing of a battery of senses is an area in which deer easily best the hunter. We're not very capable of bringing several senses to bear at once. I recently watched a whitetail buck that had heard a stick crack under my boot. Instantly it cocked its ears but didn't run. It did begin staring intently, head low, neck out, then moving its head side to side, attempting to enhance depth perception. Meanwhile, in this rigid pose, it was slowly moving, each foot precisely placed, not away but in an arc that was the shortest route to bring any available scent on the small breeze to it. All senses, after one was alerted, were being used almost as one, and with intense concentration. That's what so often licks the hunter. He should bear this in mind and keep trying to devise ways to frustrate all senses at once.

The most important facet of deer hunting lore related to their senses is the one least often considered. Granted, all three deer senses are superbly sharp. But of the sounds, sights, and scents filtered through those senses, which *disturb* the animals? Just because a deer sees, hears, or scents something doesn't necessarily mean it's scared. The hunter who ponders this and understands the difference beween sights, sounds, and scents that don't alarm deer in a given location, and those that are thoroughly disturbing to them, will wind up as the most astute and successful hunter.

Here is an example. Our homesite, which has about 25 acres of woodland behind it, is surrounded on three sides by smaller acreages with homes. Resident deer that actually live on our property but roam widely at night probably number ten to twelve each year. We often observe them. Around us dogs bark; lawn mowers and chainsaws growl; automobiles start, stop, and pass by; and voices of people are commonly audible. Deer feed and move about in their cover and along its edges with no concern whatever. I can even drive my 4-wheel-drive vehicle (4WD) back on our hills and though nearby deer run, they stop in the first copse of cover.

Now move down to our ranch, where no one lives. It's quite remote. There are several hundred acres of wild land, with no neighbor dwellings close by. A vehicle motor or chainsaw here not only alerts deer but makes them uneasy. They flee wildly when you approach them, and the human voice is a most frightening sound.

Thus, the conditions under which any given deer lives make sounds, sights, and scents more, or less, frightening at greater, or lesser, distances. I've watched mounted cowhands and pick-up trucks cover mule deer country on ranches with little disturbance to mule deer that were in sight. However, try riding in an open, short four-wheel-drive vehicle so the human face and form shows, or get down and walk and see what happens. Every deer will run. These sights and sounds are strange and aren't very tolerable.

So much hokum has been purveyed about the senses of deer that many hunters don't understand the reality. A hunter who smelled of some sweetish gunk told me last fall that he had daubed himself with apple scent because deer love apples and the smell appeals to them, thus allaying uneasiness. Various estimates place the number of deer in the U.S. at somewhere near 17 million. I'll bet not one in ten thousand of those deer has ever eaten an apple or even smelled one. For all we know, apple scent may scare the bejabbers out of those deer because they don't know what it is.

The effect of smoke on deer is another subject not always accurately portrayed. Again, much depends on what the particular deer are used to. The whitetails on my home place smell smoke commonly. Neighbors cut encroaching scrub cedar and burn it. Some burn dry trash. Although I don't smoke, I've taken a friend who did and sat in my closed vehicle, in plain sight of a feeding area where deer appear each afternoon at our home. He smoked and blew smoke purposely out the open window. Deer would look toward us, sniff, fiddle a bit, but go right on feeding afterward.

Certainly dense smoke, as in a forest fire, might alarm deer if the fire itself is close. Nevertheless, even heavy smoke drifting over deer range doesn't have any noticeable effect on deer. Cigarette smoke emanating from a hunter on a stand certainly may call attention to the area, but if the smoke drifts to the deer, you can bet hunter smell does, too. *That's* what sends the deer off with flag waving.

Consider also the matter of colors. In my early deer hunting days in the Great Lakes area, everyone wore red wool jacket and pants. I have stood immobile, gun rested against a tree, and in the open, and killed deer that were looking at me from 50 yards or so away while I was in bright-red, non-shiny wool set off against white snow. While I sat on stand, thus clad, does have walked by on still days within a few paces, taken a look at me, and continued on their way.

My own suspicion is that deer are at least nearly color blind, if not entirely. But that's not really the point. One hunter explained to me recently that a colored jacket frightens the deer. Does that mean red, for example, as a *color* frightens deer? Think of all those deer thrown into paroxysms of fear when the maples in the North turn crimson.

The results of messages brought to deer through their three senses are translated into degrees of uneasiness not so much by what they are as: where the deer live; what they are used to; how they interpret the message (dangerous or benign); how close the stimulus is; and how sustained the disturbance is. I've watched deer countless times when a distant gunshot sounded. Most of the time they don't even raise the head from feeding or give any response. However, on opening day in a crowded area, when scores of hunters invade a deer range that has been relatively undisturbed all year, and a lot of shooting and human sound and movement occurs throughout it, deer are obviously spooked. The longer this massive disturbance continues on into the season, the greater the anxiety and wild behavior of the deer. Under such conditions all rules are off.

The more the beginning deer hunter learns about how deer use their senses and how his own stack up, and the more he learns about how to use them, the better and more successful hunter he'll ultimately be. The most important rule in rating deer senses and in understanding how they're used and how you can thwart their effectiveness is to always keep in mind that deer have been conditioned to consider man as the ultimate predator. The sight of the human face, the sound of the human voice, and the human smell are anathema to deer. Of the three, the last is the most difficult to conceal.

Water, near an area difficult to get to and to get a deer out of, is almost certain to be a buck bedding area. Try to select your tract containing such a spot.

When you scout your area, note all places where you can hide and glass quickly if necessary.

CHAPTER 25
100-ACRE DEER HUNT

Ample cover is mandatory in your selection. Small spots of it, well scattered, help you quess where bucks may be.

Early in my deer hunting career I hunted the public lands of a large state forest in northern Michigan. Hunting was considered very good there. That didn't mean that every hunter got a deer every year, but bagging a buck every other year was a reasonable expectation. Overall success ran about 20 percent.

I remember that the longer the season continued without a chance for a shot, the harder I hunted. By "hard" I mean that I took off at dawn and walked all day, or as much of it as I could physically bear. I knew other deer hunters who did likewise, always thinking that maybe another mile up a ridge, along a river, or across a swamp they'd find fortune.

Reflecting on those years, I realize that a measure of one's hunting "skill" at that time and place was to some extent dependent on how much territory he covered. The more miles that went under your boots, the better the chances for success. That premise — utterly false — was the general concept of whitetail hunting then, and among a high percentage of today's deer hunters, it remains a basic tactic.

There is something else I remember all too well from those years that proves how ill-conceived the "more-miles" theory is. Between our house and the state forest boundary, I had to drive through several miles of small-farm country. These old-fashioned, family-subsistence farms ran from 60 to 160 acres. A typical farm had perhaps a third or even half of its total acreage in woods. Some had a creek with banks fringed by trees and undergrowth. Patches of low ground were grown up into "greenswamps" — balsam and cedar tangles with willow around the edges.

On one of these farms lived an old gentleman whose grandfather had cleared the land himself when all that country was virgin forest. The place contained 90 acres. Always by the third or fourth day of deer season there was a buck hanging in the old man's farmyard. On the days when I'd come home each evening exhausted and deerless and have to look at that buck, I confess I was envious.

My envy grew as I learned more about that old gentleman. During the time we lived there, he passed his 50th year of deer hunting. He celebrated it by whacking an extra-large 10-pointer. He had never failed to hang up a deer in 50 consecutive seasons — and he had never hunted deer off his own 90-acre farm.

Later I made a point of getting to know him. I've long remembered what he told me when I asked how he could be so astonishingly and consistently successful. "Why," he said, "there isn't anything so very special about it. The deer live here and so do I. Most of the bucks I've killed I suppose were born right here. So was I. They know every square foot of this farm, and so do I. You don't need a lot of territory in order to kill a deer. You just need to know a small piece as well as the deer do."

The old gentleman's advice proved a gem of deer hunting wisdom back then, but it is perhaps even more applicable to today's hunting. Almost everywhere the whitetail woods are crowded with hunters. Many hunters have the feeling that if they can cover a lot of territory fast, they will be successful and beat out the other guy. They believe that if they stay put in a small area too long, they are missing countless opportunities.

The fact is, exactly the opposite is true. When you roam widely, you have time to learn only the most general features of the terrain. You leave one buck's territory and go into that of another, and another. You never learn much about how each buck lives in its domain. In effect, you are shotgunning the country, hoping to get lucky. Using this method you never come to know any piece of deer range "as well as the deer do." And if you kill a deer, you probably *are* lucky; more than likely someone else ran it to you.

Consider for a moment what the deer are doing. Granted, during deer season all of them — most of them anyway — will get pushed around some by hunters. However, whitetails won't leave the general area where they live. They may change their habits, perhaps feeding more at night, or they may run out of their home range temporarily. But they'll come right back. Each deer or group of deer has certain favorite feeding, bedding, and hiding areas. They *live* there. In dry country each has specific watering places. In most whitetail country, however, water is seldom scarce, and deer generally are not tied to a particular stream or lake.

An individual deer feeds off and on during the night and into the dawn. This time is spent in a feeding area where forage is abundant. After feeding, the deer moves along well-defined trails to reach a bedding or hiding spot. During the middle of the day, the whitetail sticks close to these bedding areas but frequently wanders around to feed, get water, or move from one haunt to another. Late in the afternoon, the deer heads down a favorite trail and winds up back at the feeding area. The hunter's task is to intercept the deer along one of its well-defined trails, stand-hunt for the deer at the feeding area, or still-hunt for the deer in likely bedding areas.

The point to be made is that no whitetail pursues its basic routines over a vast area. Given ample food, water, and resting places, a whitetail may live out its days without traveling over more than 200 acres. At the most a whitetail will probably spend its days, during good seasons and bad, within a square mile, or a bit more.

Therefore, for those thousands of hunters who perhaps go to the same region annually, the best advice is to cease helter-skelter, long-distance hunting. First select an area where deer reside. Sign, of course, easily gives the animals away. Then, mentally or even physically mark off boundaries within which to hunt, and adamantly stay within them. Purposely keep the area small. A hundred acres is a good average. That is a bigger piece of country than most hunters realize, and it is easily an ample amount in which to kill a deer.

The measurements of 100 acres may surprise you. Each acre contains 4,840 square yards. An acre laid out in a square is roughly 70 paces — yards on the average — on each side. If you walked around the perimeter of a single acre, you would have covered almost 280 yards. To know a piece of deer range as well as the deer know it, however, not only would you have to travel the perimeter of each acre, but you also would have to crisscross each acre diligently, noting every rock, bush, dip, rise, tree, ridge, or valley.

Certainly some 100-acre tracts will sustain more deer than others. However, it is not how *many* animals are present, but how well you know their habits within this modest tract of ground — not general deer habits anywhere, but the individual habits of these particular deer on this particular piece of range.

For example, on our small Texas ranch, which contains 350 acres of very rough country, a creek with high bluffs at some places meanders down through the center of the ranch and all the way across it. We know precisely where the deer can and cannot cross. We know which rocky canyons and draws they use when going to and from the creek.

There are certain cedar brakes on ridges where we know deer always bed down, hide, or rest. There are definite escape routes which our deer will use. I think of one ridge with an open area among oaks and cedars where several dozen deer have been bagged in the 30-odd years we've owned this place.

The only way you can know the daily routine of the deer in your hunting area is by spending time in the woods, scouting for sign and learning the terrain. Even then a kill is not always easy. But it is simpler than fiddling aimlessly, trying to cover an enormous sweep of country and hoping by sheer chance to stumble on a buck. It is also more intriguing hunting. You wind up *outwitting* a deer.

There is a steep, rocky draw on our ranch that has an enormous chunk of rock lying in the center of its mouth. Prowling around the area one fall, my son noticed that deer sign was abundant and a trail leading up the draw was well worn. He noticed, too, that all the travel sign was to the *left* of that huge rock, as he faced the draw. There was ample passage room on the other side, too. But here a jumble of sharp, cubic-foot-size rocks were tumbled. These — as we doped it — were inconvenient for deer to cross. On the traveled side there was only worn shale.

Now this could have been just a casual observation and forgotten. But because we hunt this place every season for some weeks, we turned it into an important bit of knowledge. A hunter sitting to the right of the draw mouth would have only a fleeting glimpse of a deer, even a walking animal, as it moved up or down the draw. The huge rock in the center blocked the view, and the deer, we felt certain, would pass on the shale side out of habit and convenience, even if spooked and running. From that side, however, an open shot was presented for possibly 20 yards. It would be easy to pass this off as not all that important — except that since the day of this discovery four bucks have been taken there by watching that left side when wind was right. Two others walked unscathed in front of hunters who didn't listen closely enough to our instructions and who watched from the right side.

The "100-Acre Deer Hunt," as it might be called, is really a unique philosophy of deer hunting. Interestingly, a great many landowners have followed this philosophy all their lives without thinking about it. The midwestern farmer, the New England orchard owner, the Texas rancher all know the land and how the deer live on it. The average urban-dwelling deer hunter, far in the majority nowadays, of course does not have the opportunity to live with the deer year round. All the more reason why he should block out a small hunting area for himself and memorize every minute feature of it.

How do you go about selecting the proper tract for this close-focus deer study? It may sound ridiculous, but I am convinced it makes little difference which one you choose. That, too, is part of the philosophy. If there are deer on it, what more is required? Certainly a heavy population helps, but that is not overly important. What you have to fix in your mind is that you are hunting only the deer whose sign you see within your boundaries. You are hunting one, or two, or three or four bucks (or does) instead of a dozen or 20 scattered hither and yon.

A friend of mine who hunts by the 100-acre system has the right idea. "Think of it this way," he says. "When you go into the woods and see fresh deer droppings, or tracks, a couple of buck rubs on a ridge, or a scrape under a creek-bottom tree, picture yourself as right then in the center of maybe 100 acres. It is almost a sure bet, therefore, that one or more of the deer that made the sign you've seen is within that plot. And if you visualize it as a square tract, that puts the deer, at the most, only 575 yards from you, and at the closest boundary points, a mere 350 yards.

It's an intriguing way to think of it. Surely a deer that close can be tagged. It certainly can if you learn the habitat as well as *it* has. I start the process by combing the area for the most abundant foods that season. For instance, has poplar been cut in an area for pulp, and are new shoots coming up? Is there an abundance of scrub maple with low twigs? Do the oaks have a big acorn crop? What shrubs are present that bucks are most likely to use for rubs? That's a quick way to find where bucks are living. I also look for thick, remote places where deer will bed down. Then what about natural travel routes, creek crossings, and so on. If the season is one of severe drought, water may be the key to success. Are there small hidden springs or puddles? Has a rivulet dried up all but a few small puddles?

Every time I jump a deer, I note which way it runs. Wind will have a bearing on the direction, but deer not scared witless will follow certain pre-established, habitual escape routes. These are important to you. Once you know the basic features of this miniature range, it's time to get down to a finer focus. Where are the best places to sit? There may be as many as a dozen or more of them, depending on the amount of deer sign and the wind on a given day. Where are the easiest routes for you to prowl with the best chances to surprise a deer in its bed?

Of course, on public lands one can't always select exactly the tract he may want. It may not be possible to get away from the crowds. Don't let that drive you out. The resident deer won't be driven out.

As you learn the details of the tract you plan to hunt, you'll gain confidence in your ability to outsmart a buck. I don't claim that big bucks will always become easy to gather. But any hunter who'll stake out 100 acres as well as the deer do stands a better chance of killing a deer every season than the hunter who roams all over the woods and lets luck do his hunting for him.

When a snowstorm hits during moderate weather deer often seem to disappear. These hunters head in after discovering that.

Hard hunting might find a deer on a day when the snow ceases falling, but you can save much work by waiting for a bright post-storm day.

CHAPTER 26
HOPE FOR A STORM

After a severe storm, with snow melted, deer seem to pop out of the ground.

My deer hunting begn a good many years ago in the big-woods country of northern Michigan during a period when a deer camp was usually
a weather-flogged old wall tent banked with fallen leaves mixed with
the dirt dug from trenching around it, and the mattresses inside along
the walls were pallets of straw. I remember vividly how everyone hoped
for a slight ground covering of snow for opening day — tracking snow,
they called it — but almost everyone was uneasy about the possibility
of a big early storm. The resulting weather would most certainly shut
off deer activity like the turn of a spigot.

Camped each fall way up a long-unused logging road on the Pigeon
River, however, were an old man and his two grown sons. They were
farmers from somewhere downstate who always came in an ancient
truck and didn't worry about storms. I hunted a section of forest that
took me past their camp several times, and the old gent would always
insist I pause for a cup of coffee. What I remember most about him
is that he never fussed about the possibility that a furious blizzard might
hit. Instead, he always hoped one would.

Holding his chipped graniteware coffee cup in both gnarled hands
to warm them, he smiled through seventy years of accumulated
wrinkles one day and told me, "Sure, a bad one'll ruin the hunting for
a day or two. That just gives you a fine chance to lie around camp cozy-
warm and anticipate what'll come after. Any young fellow — like you
— should learn that early. A storm's the best that can happen. Afterward the meat pole fills up quick."

I tucked away this oddment of lore and have used it to advantage
on numerous occasions. It's true that I've cozied out, shivered out, worried out, and even starved out storms during deer seasons in several
states when I fervently wished I was anywhere but where I was. On the
other hand, I cannot recall a single time when, having waited for the
weather switch, the action was anything but great. And every time I
gave up and went home in disgust, as many hunters do annually, I had
to listen afterward to the big-buck tales of those who'd stuck it out.

In many parts of the country, deer seasons fall during a time when
weather is whimsical. As Indian summer wanes and real fall begins,
the progression of seasons is triggered by drastic changes in the
weather. Sometimes fall slides along into winter with a steady, pleasant-
ly innocuous pace. Much of the time, however, intermittent storms give
rowdy foretastes of winter with respites in between. Those are the times!

Deer dislike severe storms and the erratic changes they bring, just
as hunters do. Certainly deer are not as drastically affected by mild

changes. They live out in the weather constantly, and to them a driz-zle of rain, a light filtering of snow, a moderately chilly freeze is just another day. A fall-fat deer, in fact, seeks a shady spot, even a bed out of the sun on a patch of early snow, on days when a hunter will pull on his longjohns. Nonetheless, when a real whistler moves in, deer seek comfort and protection. Deer activity as well as most hunter ac-tivity shuts down for the duration of the storm.

What disturbs the animals most is high wind. They can't hear well in it. Branches and trees are noisy; everything is moving, even the grass. It's difficult for them to discern which movements may and may not be signs of danger.

Furthermore, especially in hilly or mountainous country, a strong wind blows — as oldhand hunters say — "from seven directions at once." To a deer, this means that the direction from which disturbing scents are coming can't be reliably pinned down. Thus, for safety as well as comfort, the deer go into hiding.

Few substantial storms during deer season, however, are just high wind. Rain, sleet, snow, or a combination usually come too. In the high-country West, mule deer forage on north slopes may be covered with deep snow. The same may occur in the flatter ranges of the whitetail. But deer hunters should not equate lack of deer movement only with deep snow piled by a bitter wind. In fact, throughout all U.S. deer ranges that are usually without snow, deer are even more disturbed by an abrupt change to a bitter wind with or without light snow, sleet, or rain than they are by somewhat more severe fall storms in the North. For some years now, for example, I have hunted for desert mule deer in the Southwest in late November. Sometimes it's downright hot. But every year or so a "most unusual" snowstorm hits the desert moun-tains at that time.

Even though the temperature plummets, the snow may not amount to anything more than a couple of inches. The winds, though, are in-variably vicious. During such times you can drive the ranch trails all day and swear there's not a single deer to a hundred thousand acres. I've seen swarms of hunters pull out for home, frustrated and mutter-ing — same as in every state every season when a hard storm strikes. Some are afraid of getting snowed in. Some, because they're in strange country, are convinced the horrible weather will last for weeks.

Seldom, however, do those early-winter storms last very long. There may be just three or four days before the lull comes. Just wait until that first crisp, still dawn arrives, with blue sky and bright sun.

You'll see deer practically pop out of the ground. One November on the desert mule deer range, a companion and I were driving ranch trails on the first clear day after a spell of blizzards, and we counted over 200 deer!

Keep in mind that the timing of deer seasons usually coincides with a period when the daily lives of deer are undergoing dramatic seasonal changes anyway, regardless of unsettled weather. Their forage is changing drastically. Growing season has ceased, frosts are killing much green vegetation, and acorns are ripening — if there's a crop — and falling. New travel patterns are forced on the animals in their search for food.

Additionally, this is the time of the rut. Whether the peak of the rut falls during the season where you hunt is not as important as the fact that the entire rut overlaps several fall and winter months, so some activity is evident during most hunting seasons. But a severe storm will interfere with the rut, as well as with feeding patterns.

Depending on the severity of the storm, and how long it hangs on, deer have either fed poorly or not at all. When the front has moved through, leaving a clearing sky and usually a rising barometer, hungry deer swarm from hiding, intent on filling their bellies. From the hunter's viewpoint they are now most vulnerable.

In any area where a storm has brought deep and drifting snow, deer will head for the places where they know they can most easily obtain the most forage quickly and with the least effort. They also have an uncanny instinct for the most nutritious, high-protein items available, assuming that forage is not scarce.

In my area, and eastward across much of the South, numerous farmers and ranchers plant fields of winter oats or wheat. By deer season many of these crops are well sprouted. Here is succulent green forage long after comparable wild food is gone. After a spate of tough weather, whitetails simply crowd along the edges of these patches. During years when there is a heavy nut crop in the several Western states where piñon trees are present, mule deer following a storm will dot the southern slopes where the trees grow and where the snow has not extensively collected, grubbing for the sweet nuts on the ground and even knocking them out of cones on low branches.

In the North, an early storm, or even several, won't send whitetails into "yards." Yarding occurs only when snow becomes so deep the deer can't travel in it. Likewise, the first big blow or two won't necessarily send mountain mule deer down from their high summer ranges in places where they make vertical migrations to winter range. After the weather subsides they'll home in on the stands of mountain mahogany and aspen and similar browse.

When truly heavy snow piles up, however, they'll move down. Yet the majority of these migrating deer sense that they're better off to stay put — and hungry — until the big blow subsides. Then they start the trek. I hunted in Colorado one fall when a tremendous snow hit the mountains on opening day. We were camped in an old, remote cow camp cabin at around 8,000 feet. Several of the group, disturbed and afraid they'd be there all winter, made a desperate and rather foolish effort to get out, and after much difficulty did. The rest of us ate, slept, tippled a bit, listened to the pack rats, and waited it out.

A bright sun and rising temperature and barometer had the snow melting on the third day. When horses could travel with careful handling, several of us rode part way up the backdrop mountain. The scene was amazing. Mule deer were in sight just everywhere, a few drifting down to lower country, most filling their bellies on shinoak brush, the most abundant and nutritious forage in the area. A jackpot. You could almost literally pick out the one you liked best.

Becoming familiar with the abundant and most nutritious protein sources in his hunting region is what puts a hunter on the firing line after a storm. During sustained gentle weather either whitetails or mule deer may wander, feeding on a variety of tidbits. But when the lull after the big storm turns deer out of their corrals, they don't dally. Whatever is tastiest, quickest, and most bountiful is what they'll head for. En route or at their destination, they're easy to collect.

Also following a storm, both species of deer are inclined to be in the open more than previously, and in the sunshine, at least for the first day. This is, of course, most noticeable with whitetails, for mule deer are creatures of more open country anyway. One fall when Peter Barrett of *Field & Stream* and I were hunting whitetails along the Mexican border in Texas, our trip coincided with rain and nasty, bitter wind whistling out of the northwest. It persisted for several days. In the famed trophy-deer brush country here, where our guide John Finegan knew deer were superbly abundant, we cruised ranch trails for hours without seeing a hair. Although Pete did fill his tags by diligent effort of all concerned, the day after he went back to New York the wind died, the sun shone, and, so Finegan told me, deer appeared all over the ridges.

Of course if you're tough enough, love to suffer, and can do it with grace, there is an alternative to waiting out the storm. A crafty prowler can do almost as well during the bad spell as after. In rugged Western mountains it may not be possible to get around. But in most whitetail country and the lower mule deer ranges, the majority of storms won't totally prohibit hunter action. This is, as my west Texas rancher friend would say, "hunting *in* the corral." It is not difficult to predict where deer will be, and they are often concentrated. Wherever they can get the most protection and comfort — just like the hunters lazing it out in cabin or tent — is where they'll put up.

In my early days, when storms weren't as severe as they have become nor hills as steep, and a mile against the knife-edged wind measured about half what it does nowadays, a friend and I took delight in going into the greenswamps after deer when the blizzard was on. Deep in the cedars and balsams, storm noise was diminished. None but tracks so fresh you could almost smell them were imprinted in accumulating snow, and a careful operator could sneak up — as we did on occasion — on a buck in its hideaway. The storm was our ally.

Several years ago during a vile storm in the Southwest, I rode along miles of trails with a cowboy who took care of windmills on a huge cattle ranch. He knew the trails intimately. We were after mule deer and paid no attention to any but the southern and southeastern exposures, where the wind and the fine blowing sleet were to some extent cut off. Visibility was difficult, but we finally found a pair of ten-point bucks bedded comfortably among rocks high on a slope.

One fall from the comfort of a vehicle and with my gun cased, I watched two vigorous and eager Easterners get out time after time to walk with their guide along steep, narrow, south-running brush-choked draws cutting from ridges down toward the U.S. side of the Rio Grande River. Anyone who thinks the Mexican border can't be cold when a norther hits has never been there when one did. Those dudes muttered and cussed, bundled in down. Nonetheless they jumped deer after deer out of those wait-out havens, missed several prime bucks, but also laid two on the ground.

Nowadays I do my hunting when the lull comes, still using the advice of the old Michigan farmer. Whether you elect to hunt during or after, a rousing deer-season storm is to be hoped for, not worried over. It can be a tag-filler for those who stick it out.

A chattering squirrel may mean it has seen you, seen a deer, or seen another hunter — or perhaps it's chattering because it feels like it.

Some "experts" may tell you if you see numerous does, bucks will be nearby. During the rut that may be true. At other times get away from the does to find a good buck.

CHAPTER 27
DEER HUNTING MALARKEY

Are tracks those of a buck? It's extremely doubtful that anyone can be certain.

When a sport is as popular as deer hunting, it is certain to be endlessly discussed and documented. I've been deer hunting for more than fifty years, and I've read, as well as written, a lot of words about the sport. I've also heard a lot of deer hunting lore and first-person stories over the years. Kiddingly I tell friends that each deer season I hear at least ten thousand "How I Bagged My Buck" tales, most of them with profound revelations of brilliant tricks employed by the hunter to clinch success. As I listen, I always make sure my salt shaker is at hand.

Certainly an awesome amount of authentic information about the how-to of deer hunting, and the habits and abilities of the animals, has been handed down over the years. But among it are bits and pieces all of us endlessly repeat among ourselves and pass along to beginners, nice pat little gems, some of them really delightful nuggets of lore, that we never question. Are they all true? Or are some, at least in part, pure old malarkey?

Consider, for example, the old saw about jays and squirrels, and how when one or the other, or both, begin to jabber, that tells the hunter on his stand a deer is coming. Sometimes this one is reversed, and the jabbering tells the deer that a hunter is coming. Thousands of boys after their first buck have accepted this gospel from their dads or granddads, or have learned it from the writings of some expert, who picked it up no doubt from the writings of some other expert — ad infinitum. The young fellows listen, as do their dads, for that tattletale jay or squirrel. It's a good feeling to know you are equipped with such sneaky lore, isn't it? But does anyone ever wonder if it's true?

On our place in the country we have whitetails, fox squirrels, and Texas scrub jays. I have a wonderful opportunity to watch them all year. In addition, I've hunted where mule deer and big Steller's jays share habitat, where camp robber jays, crested bluejays, and other jays were present, and where gray squirrels, red squirrels, and pine squirrels also lived with deer. The jays screech at each other, at other birds, and often out of what appears to be pure exuberance or cussedness, whenever they feel like it. The squirrels chatter at each other, sometimes at the jays. But squirrels are by no means as vocal as most hunters believe they are, especially during the time of year when most deer seasons fall. Neither squirrels nor jays pay much attention to deer.

In our yard in fall I often can watch whitetails eating fallen acorns beneath a live oak. Commonly a fox squirrel scurries out among them. Neither pays any attention to the other. I've often seen a squirrel run under the belly of a feeding deer. No reaction from either. Suddenly a big scrub jay swoops in. Sometimes it yelps, sometimes not. Jays also like acorns. A jay will fly off with one, break it open, eat part of the meat, sometimes joyously cussing meanwhile. If I appear distantly, none of these creatures says anything. They simply leave.

Now I'm not saying that a jay or squirrel never jabbers at a hunter or a deer, but the infallible gospel about their warnings, though pleasant enough in the passing along, is just plain malarkey. Unfortunately, deer hunting lore is all too loaded with such "truths."

The trouble with swallowing the malarkey along with legitimate lore is that you inhibit your own progress toward becoming a truly expert deer hunter. To be sure, it's often difficult to separate the authentic, because so much that is dubious is also at least partly true. For example, there's the matter of distinguishing between buck tracks and doe tracks. You'll hear that the buck is heavier and sinks in farther; that it drags its feet; and that the toes of an old buck are rounded. These are supposed to be sure signs that the tracks you are following belong to a buck.

Unfortunately, the consensus among the best authorities on tracking is that there's no infallible way to tell the sex of a deer by its tracks. *Some* bucks are heavier. *Some* bucks drag their feet. But that's not always the case. Some seasons ago a track expert friend led me along the trail of what he said was a tremendous buck — but that turned out to be an ancient, fat, splay-footed doe. Certainly if you see tracks of two small deer and one larger one, you can guess that probably a doe and twin fawns made them. And deer tracks of any sort do indicate that deer are in the area. But other than that, tracks are not especially useful to the average hunter and are the least useful sign to anyone looking for a buck.

Don't mistake me — malarkey is kind of nice to have, in modest amounts. Some of the tidbits are at least good for laughs. In my state rattling up whitetail bucks during the rut by whacking together a pair of antlers sawed from a skull is a popular and effective method of bringing bucks to the gun. I've done a lot of it. Other rattlers invariably like to examine the rattling antlers I use. On three different occasions I've had an "expert" ask me if I am aware of the curious fact that it's impossible to rattle up a whitetail buck if you use mule deer antlers. It just happens that the pair I use — quite successfully at times — came from a mule deer. No special reason, except they're the right size and conformation to handle easily. They work, too, although according to my informants, they shouldn't.

There's also the malarkey about the barren doe. With most states now encouraging the taking, under permits, of antlerless deer to assist herd control, numerous hunters claim they always select a barren doe. That way, they say, they're sure to get a fat one. And she's out of the fawn business so they aren't inhibiting production. It's not inconceivable that a hunter may by chance shoot a barren doe. But purposely? Even highly trained biologists have difficulty identifying barren does. The most amusing incident I know of relative to the barren doe malarkey concerns a friend who selected such a doe, shot it — and picked up an old out-of-business buck.

Some of the nonsense represented as fact wastes much time and effort besides giving hunters bum steers. Recently I read detailed instructions about how a deer hunter should plan a combination summer vacation and scouting trip in the area where he'll hunt deer the following fall. It described how to locate feeding places, trails, and bedding areas, and discern general daily habits of deer in the area, so when the season opens, the hunter's intercept spots already will be established.

That's utter nonsense and probably the worst advice ever concocted, an excellent road to confusion and an unfilled tag. Many summer-used deer trails are abandoned by the time the season arrives. Mainstays of diet have drastically changed, and with them, of course, favored feeding places and deer movements. Weather and resultant fall changes in cover may even rearrange bedding locations. The rut may be on when you hunt, which breaks up normal deer routines. The only advantage of summer scouting on your deer-hunt area, so far as fall hunting is concerned, is in established generalities about the deer population.

Because the whitetail deer, in particular, ranges so widely and in such a variety of terrain, undoubtedly the all-time classic of muddled up malarkey concerns its food. Make no mistake, eating is the most important function of a deer's day, as far as the hunter is concerned. The times when a deer is filling its stomach or moving to and from forage are the times when hunters get most of their opportunities. Thus, knowing what deer eat is vitally important.

I have on my bookshelf thirteen volumes, by actual count, that insist whitetails love apples above all other foods. Just find an abandoned or woods-edge apple orchard and success is assured. A close check shows all these books were written by people whose experience was restricted almost entirely to the East. Yet other writers parrot this nonsense endlessly. Come now, doesn't it sound a little bit silly? It is true that whitetails like apples, but only where and when apples are readily available. But in much of the vast area where whitetails live, the deer never see or smell an apple. For all I know, in the swamps of Louisiana, the thornbrush of southern Texas, or the forests of eastern Wyoming, the smell of apples might *frighten* whitetail deer.

The apple business — even the ads for apple scents claiming they're great because "deer love apples" — is a ridiculous attempt to apply to all whitetail range what happens chiefly in only a few isolated parts. Deer love corn, too — in some places. But I helped carry hundreds of pounds of corn one year out into the southwestern cactus country to put into deer feeders for whitetails as a supplementary feed experiment the landowners were doing. The deer wouldn't touch it at first, and it was months before they began gingerly testing it. The moral here is that hunters should forget generalities and look for the favorite deer foods when and where they are hunting. For example, muleys and whitetails along the Mexican border love the base sections of sotol and lechuguilla leaves. Try hunting patches of those in apple country!

A number of set-in-concrete "facts" about deer hunting passed down through many generations are not only plain hokum, but are harmful hokum to boot. For example, there's the one about how wounded whitetails run off with the tail held close, not raised. The truth is, no tail-language rule applies.

Some wounded whitetails run with the tail held tight down against the rear. Others do the opposite. Once in northern Michigan a friend I was hunting with shot a running buck at close range. The deer's tail was up when he shot. The buck didn't even flinch. The last we saw of it, it was going all out with tail high. We walked up on it 10 minutes later, dead. We'd seen a small dribble of blood on snow. Conversely, on countless occasions, I have watched whitetails I knew were not hit — a fact proved by finding where the bullet had gone — yet the fleeing deer kept its tail snugly down. This is a fairly common whitetail sneak-away trick. The malarkey about tail position and wounded deer argues strongly for using restraint, picking your shot opportunities for clean kills, and diligently following up *any* deer shot at and presumably missed.

Deer-camp discussions invariably come around to expansive tales of the craftiness of the quarry, and this is certain to prompt someone to expound on the marvels of deer intelligence and their infallible senses. "Mark my word,'" the Oldhand admonishes the Tyro, "deer are smart. They don't make mistakes." This is classic malarkey. Deer are indeed intelligent. But during an average season about 1 ¾ million of them make fatal mistakes. We deer hunters would be out of business if they didn't.

Over the past decade the idea of hunting from a tree stand or high blind has boomed in popularity. It has lately been heavily touted as the only sure way to keep deer from becoming aware of you. There's no question that an above-ground stand greatly decreases chances of hunter discovery by the deer. But enthusiasm for the method also has nurtured lots of nonsense about it. I just read a magazine article explaining that a tree stand or high seat of any sort guarantees that deer in the vicinity will neither see nor scent a hunter.

Don't you believe it! I live in and hunt the Hill Country of Texas, where the high blind saw unique development as much as half a century ago. Deer on many ranches there stand off at a distance and stare at permanent high blinds or trees that have had seats in them every season for years, checking for occupancy. A deer knows its domain down to the last bush. In areas where they are heavily hunted from above, deer get to cocking a glance upward at any suspicious bundle.

The oft repeated wheeze about how a deer's physical build prevents it from looking up is at least half malarkey too. Deer can't look up quite as steeply as a man can. And, they don't look up constantly, because there's no need to. However, even at fifty paces a deer easily sees a man 15 feet up in a tree, if its attention is alerted, because even at that range the angle is shallow. I know a rancher who feeds deer in his yard, and who has fooled with one buck until it catches cubes of livestock feed tossed into the air. It tosses its head back, darts forward and grabs the cube as it falls. That buck's build doesn't inhibit it from looking up!

Deer also quickly scent a hunter in a high blind or stand if they happen to be downwind at a distance. When we first moved to Texas and I had my first high stand experiences, I felt pretty smug, until I observed deer crossing as much as 300 yards downwind of me. Especially if the wind was gusty, every one would suddenly whirl, stare toward where I sat, test the air, then flee wildly. They obviously were picking up a downwind flow of settling scent.

Sages of the deer woods endlessly explain to the neophytes how only the early and late hunting hours are worthwhile for putting meat on the pole. They usually do this while lying around camp in the middle of the day. The neophyte shouldn't be there listening. He should be out hunting. Contrary to old hokum, deer do have minor activity periods during the day, and can be caught at it if you too are on your feet. Many of these same purveyors of half truths are the ones who still stick a dead deer first thing, or cut its throat, instead of bleeding it by simply field dressing it. I've also been told by several old-legend tellers that hanging a field-dressed deer in camp by the antlers will ruin the hams. Allows blood to drain down into them over a period of hours, they say. Skin a deer sometime with it lying out flat, as on a pickup tailgate, immediately after gutting. Then hang it by the head and saw through the backbone just above the hams, thus removing both hams. There won't be a tablespoon of blood that drips from the remainder of the carcass regardless of how long it hangs.

It's not just the old legends and beliefs that need to be taken with a grain of salt. Scientists continue to learn more and more about deer, and much of this new knowledge eventually filters down through the written word to the hunter in the field. Certainly everyone should be willing to accept advances in learning. A problem arises, however, when the learner adds conjecture of his own.

Much has been made in print of the fact that deer have been discovered to have rather poor depth perception. The idea is not new, but has recently been seized upon by outdoor journalists, some of whom have pointed out that this is what causes deer to have accidents — especially getting caught in fences. Here the new learning is forced by pure conjecture over into the domain of hokum. How many times have you watched a spooked deer running all-out through heavy cover, bounding over bushes, dodging among saplings, skirting rocks, with never a stumble or bobble? Does such adept performance indicate a sight-impaired creature groping its way? If deer depth perception was all that bad, every third animal would have a broken leg.

Deer are among the most successful colonizers on earth. They haven't accomplished such broad adaptation to varying habitats by bumbling into things and being especially accident prone. A deer on its home range knows every foot of it intimately. Before a farmer or rancher can get a fence built, the resident deer know precisely where it is. I have opportunity almost daily to watch deer on my own place sail over fences. Some crawl through between barbwire strands habitually, or crawl under at a low spot. I've seen one race at a fence, drop flat to the ground, and duck under a lower strand where only a 14-inch space (measured) was available. And they can do it — zip — and be gone. Such performances hardly indicate an animal seriously handicapped with sight problems. Their depth perception may differ from ours — but how and to what degree? Nobody really knows.

There's no doubt that the malarkey you hear about deer and deer hunting isn't going to disappear. But serious deer hunters can help themselves become better hunters and better deer managers by keeping the salt handy, and by weighing the old commandments for both truth and hokum content. The proof of the wisdom offered by many a questionable expert often is nothing more than the fact that by gad he's been hunting deer for half a century and he's always known that. But maybe for half a century that "expert" has been wrong!

Jim Hayne, partner in a large, Big Bend region ranch, considers whether or not to tag this mule deer. They're easier than the whitetails because they frequent areas of meager cover.

Hunter John Casey during Big Bend combo deer hunt, with Texas whitetail. They're more difficult than the mule deer.

CHAPTER 28
THE COMBO DEER HUNT

If you're lucky and adept you may even collect a Carmen Mts. whitetail.

A fresh approach to deer hunting not commonly considered is a whitetail-mule deer combination hunt. Both species are present in several states. These include Washington, Montana, Wyoming, the Dakotas, Nebraska, a small portion of Kansas, western Oklahoma, Texas. Two-deer bag limits are not usually offered by most of these states. In Texas, however, both species have for some years been legal on the same license. Texas has upwards of 4 million deer, the most of any state. These are chiefly whitetails, with mule deer in a number of the western counties. It is possible to arrange a hunt so that you may take, most seasons currently, as many as four deer. Several seasons I have taken two whitetail bucks (or does, or one of each), plus one mule deer buck, and one mule deer doe. In certain western counties, mule deer and whitetails are both present. Thus this chapter deals with combination hunting specifically in Texas. Some seasons you may find such a hunt elsewhere. This will give you an idea of what it's like, and how to go about making arrangements.

It was not an advantageous morning for deer hunting. As we left the ranch headquarters, high-piled fog hugged the ground. My partner drove the pickup, groping without lights up a ranch trail to atop a hill, hoping to get above the fog.

Here a gentle breeze was shifting it around. The road cleared momentarily and a good whitetail buck drifted across. We quickly stopped, and I got out, making a hurried circle to try to head the deer. Presently I stood listening and heard a rock clink. Breeze curled streamers of fog across the hillside, and in a ragged opening of it the buck, head up, also listening, clothed only lightly in the gray cloud, stood broadside.

I raised my rifle, the usual prickles running up my spine. As I carefully centered on the rib cage, a puff of breeze pushed a blanket of fog between us. The buck blew loudly and was gone.

That might sound like an incident from the Texas Hill Country. Actually it occurred in northern Brewster County in the Big Bend country of the Trans-Pecos — far west Texas. Not many Texas deer hunters would think of that region as a provocative choice for a whitetail hunt. However, on that occasion I was hunting not just for a whitetail buck. I was on what might be called a double-barrelled deer hunt, hoping to tag two bucks — a whitetail and a mule deer.

That was one of several such hunts I've made. None has been easy, but all are among the most dramatic deer hunts I've ever experienced. Few deer hunters may be aware of the opportunities available for planning a two-species Texas deer hunt. If you check carefully through the game regulations booklet, you'll discover that over 40 counties have open seasons for both deer.

The mule deer season in all of them is much shorter than the whitetail season. Usually it falls in late November and runs into early December, two weeks or a bit more, while whitetails may be hunted as in much of the state, from early November into early January. Thus it's necessary to plan a two-deer hunt so it falls within mule deer season. Some of the counties where both species are legal are located west of the Pecos River, and outside it bordering the east bank of the river, or divided by it. More are in the Panhandle, and south of it in the vicinities of Lubbock and Midland.

It's important to check county regulations with care before making plans. For example, several Trans-Pecos counties have a mule deer season, but either have no whitetails or else too few to allow open season. In addition, deer limits may differ in certain counties. In some two mule deer are legal, but one must be a doe, and in some instances a doe permit is needed, from the land owner.

On two occasions I hunted in the Trans-Pecos region and collected three deer. On one ranch the land owner was anxious to cut down the mule deer doe population. We are extremely fond of desert mule deer venison. That's the subspecies found in the Big Bend country. I tagged a carefully selected doe. Then on another ranch where I was fortunate enough to have an invitation, I shot a buck mule deer. That accomplished, I concentrated on whitetails.

They're always more difficult than mule deer. Much of the difference is because the mule deer tend to stick to the open lower country. The whitetails, as everywhere they range, invariably avail themselves of cover. This places them as a rule at somewhat higher elevations and always in enough timber — oak, madrone, heavy juniper and varied brush — where they're hard to spot at any distance, easy to spook, and usually in tough-shot situations. On that three-deer hunt I got lucky, downing a heavy antlered eight pointer.

That foggy morning in Brewster County started me off on an exasperating but exciting hunt. By midday the fog cleared and the sun was out. We eased off for a couple of lunchtime hours, then decided to try for a mule deer. They were out in force by 4 p.m. A dandy 10-point made the error of bounding up a slope, then short of the top stopping, as mule deer often do, to see what spooked it. A 100 grain .243 handload put it instantly down.

I couldn't get that 8-point fog shrouded whitetail out of mind. Where I'd seen it a deep, broad wash with dense cover along its banks ran up into higher timber. Was it possible the buck lived in this area and used that wash as a travel route? I decided to hunt it.

That decision was indeed the "luck of the draw." I selected a spot where I could closely glass the timber edge and the entry to the wash within it. On either side, where I sat, there were fairly open slopes. With the sun on its way down I saw a deer move at the edge of the timber, possibly 400 yards away. I moved to the edge of the wash, concealed myself in cover. Within 20 minutes a buck I suspected was the one from the fog came tripping alertly down the open wash bottom. Again the .243 spoke sharply. That double-barrelled deer hunt was concluded.

The desert mule deer, as I've noted, is the subspecies found in far western Texas. Historically, the Rocky Mountain mule deer, the type species, ranged southeastward from its Rockies domain into the north-western part of the Texas Panhandle. There is some evidence that its historic range reached eastward much farther than is generally supposed. It was partial to the canyons, large and small, but was presumably present over a substantial expanse of the high plains.

Settlement soon reduced the range, and eventually the deer became very scarce even in the prime canyon habitat. Desert mule deer from the Trans-Pecos were transplanted there. Probably today's Panhandle mule deer are close to the full blooded desert subspecies. However, a number of unusually large-antlered deer are taken annually in the Panhandle. I've seen several heads from there with long brow tines. This is often typical of Rocky Mountain mule deer, whereas the desert subspecies typically has either very short brow tines, or none. Its skull measurements also are less. Incidentally, there is no separate desert mule deer category in Boone & Crockett records. Safari Club International, however, does place them in a separate category, which has a number of Texas deer listed.

I've heard hunters claim that the whitetails in western Texas are a regional subspecies. The fact is, they're the Texas whitetail, the same subspecies as those to the east. The Panhandle turns out a fair number of excellent heads. I've never seen specimens from the Trans-Pecos that were startling, but have collected several that certainly gave me satisfying excitement and were in the "mounting" class.

These whitetails, incidentally, should not be confused with the little Carmen Mountains subspecies, which *Texas Fish & Game* covered in an earlier story. Those diminutive whitetails are not generally abundant, and cling to the higher timbered elevations of a few Big Bend region small mountain ranges. The Texas whitetail is much more common, where there's suitable cover, and almost always at lower elevations. Wherever they occur, areas of oak often point you to them. I recall a photos-only three days I spent on a ranch north of Marathon where the oak-covered tops of several ridges, bereft of mule deer, were home to more Texas whitetails, I'm sure, than their range could sustain.

The fact that the whitetail is such an astonishingly successful and determined colonizer has caused problems for it in the Big Bend region. Most ranchers don't like them. The mule deer has long been the more abundant and readily seen. Many landowners feel that whitetails don't belong there. They worry that persistent whitetail incursion will overrun the range and somehow deplete the mule deer. Some other states have this same situation, for example, portions of Wyoming and Montana.

Further, hunters from throughout Texas have focused for years on the Trans-Pecos, and to a lesser extent the Panhandle, as the place to go instate for mule deer. Ranches where whitetails also abound have difficulty getting hunters to shoot them. Everyone wants mule deer, and plans to hunt whitetails "back home." In fact, I hunted as a guest for several years on a Trans-Pecos ranch where the owner strongly suggested we should try for a whitetail and leave the mulies alone. He wanted to whittle them down. Prospective hunters might take a hint from this. You may be able to wangle a hunt by agreeing to take one or more whitetails (where legal) along with a mule deer.

The situation in the Panhandle and southward is somewhat different. Here the preponderance of the mule deer dwell in and along the canyons and rough areas. Palo Duro Canyon and tributary canyons such as Tule Creek are the prime mule deer range. Whitetails live in wooded areas or along stream courses where there is cover, and feed out into cropland edges.

Thus the two species are more distinctly separated. South of the Panhandle some areas are basically whitetail range with small pockets amenable to mule deer. An excellent plan for Panhandle combo hunting is to arrange two different hunts, one for canyon and vicinity mule deer, another in normal whitetail habitat where few or no mule deer are present.

I sampled this one fall a few years ago. With a guide who concentrated on aoudad and mule deer in the canyons, I glassed deer from the canyon edge several evenings as they fed on their favorite shinoak browse on a canyon slope. I confess that those deer presented me with one exasperation after another. Several with antlers that got my adrenalin up evaded letting me put them down. With time running out, I settled for a rolling-fat forkhorn, then went on my whitetail hunt more successfully in another county.

As every Texas deer hunter knows, arranging any deer hunt in the state is not easy, unless you own the land. Setting up a combo hunt is more difficult, because of the hordes of sportsmen who have a fix on mule deer. Some land owners don't want to bother with hunters before or after the short mule deer season. Further, whitetails require harder, and often longer, hunting. Nevertheless, the thrill of a two-species Texas hunt is so appealing that it's worth a lot of scheming and plotting, even worth what may be a stiff price.

There are guides in both areas who may be helpful. The Texas Parks & Wildlife listing of land owners who want hunters is another source. Contacting Chambers of Commerce in the larger cities of the regions also may lead you to a hunt. Check also the Type I and Type II hunting tracts now leased or owned by TP&WD. You may find one, especially as this program grows, where both deer species are present.

There is another approach that may get surprising results. Take a classified ad in one of the newspapers in the Trans-Pecos or the other regions. State that you, and whoever will be with you, are seeking a combo deer hunt, list your telephone, collect call.

One year I booked a mule deer hunt for opening of that season, but arranged with the land owner to let me arrive several days early to hunt whitetails. This plan, either prior to or near the end of mule deer season has advantages for both rancher and hunter. It doesn't interfere with the usual concentration of fee hunters after mule deer. It gives you better opportunity with the more difficult whitetail.

However you manage it, and regardless of the difficulties involved, a west-Texas combo deer hunt is an experience tailor made for a lifetime of remembrances — and retelling.

Author's son Mike at age 11 gets his first chance at a nice whitetail buck. Meticulous training molds youngsters into calm and restrained hunters.

Author's son Terry was restricted to does and specified shot placement at first. Here he's proud of his first buck taken by carefully placed neck shot.

CHAPTER 29
THE MAKING OF A DEER HUNTER

Terry and Mike grew to be my favorite deer hunting companions. I took pride in the success of my training. Here we have a midmorning coffee break during hunt.

Yellow sunlight filtering through a gentle breeze made the pale grass shimmer. I watched the careful progress of guide Jim Barbee and my son Terry across the canyon. It was deer season, 1977, and though Terry, then 23, had taken more whitetails than most hunters his age, this was his first mule deer hunt. The location was the Davis Mountains area of western Texas.

Although I had hunted several times with Barbee, he and Terry had just met that morning. It amused me to recall how Barbee had questioned him, measuring his ability, but keeping it light.

"You shoot all right, Terry, or like your Dad?"

"Well," Terry replied, grinning, "he taught me a long time ago. I manage."

I saw them, from my parallel position 70 yards off, stop and raise their glasses. Then they were trotting, hunkered over. Slipping through a scrub thicket down on hands and knees, they slowly moved up behind a huge boulder. Terry had his rifle down, trying to get his left hand solidly between the forearm and the rock. Jim eased off his Western hat and slid it to him. Understanding, Terry tucked it under the barrel.

For a few seconds I tried to capsule my feelings. I realized I had no qualms about what sort of a deer they were seeing. Terry had told Barbee it would be a fair buck or nothing during our short stay. Nor was I worried about the shot. If it wasn't suitably presented, Terry would hold fire. I knew all that, and it felt good. It wasn't even like watching my own son. I was observing two very competent, polished deer hunters, suspended in that heady split-second before the climax. In an instant the scene seemed to dissolve and refocus, and I was way back there, 13 seasons earlier. Terry was 10 years old, another place, another deer — the first. . . .

I had carried the gun that day. Terry had been shooting targets for some time, but a deer rifle is long and heavy for a small boy. I didn't want him punching the barrel into the ground. Sure, some would say, perhaps with logic, that 10 is too young to start deer hunting. The problem was the Texas law then, or rather, the lack of it.

Our two boys, Mike and Terry, were moved to Texas when very young. Whitetails were unbelievably abundant, and country and small-town kids started hunting early. Some states require that a youngster be a certain age before hunting big game. Texas kids can legally start any time, but now only with an adult licensed hunter, unless they have taken the mandatory state hunter education course. Some Texans bragged then of holding the rifle for Junior to whomp his first deer

THE MAKING OF A DEER HUNTER

at four! I was not that anxious. In fact, I was disturbed over the intense peer pressure at school. Kids of eight or nine would tell of tagging a buck before school on opening day of deer season. Harassed but cautious, I let Mike start at age 11. By the time Terry, four years younger, reached 10, even his brother was pressuring me.

I warn parents who start children hunting big game that it is a responsibility not to be lightly shouldered. Make no mistake, how the kids mature — good or bad — is strictly up to the tutor. If you're an inept or slob deer hunter, you know it and your kids will, and they'll probably be worse. My greatest gratification is that of all the people I hunt with, I enjoy most and feel most secure with my grown offspring. I am comfortable in the knowledge of having instilled in them the philosophy of deer hunting as craftsmanship, not just killing animals.

I still chuckle when I remember that first deer of Terry's. Second kids sometimes get short-changed, so I had determined he'd have as much attention and tutoring as Mike had. We saw the deer standing unaware at perhaps 75 yards. It was a doe, and we had doe permits. I was listening to Terry breathe, and I knew the fact that it was a doe mattered not at all. We were behind a big cedar blowdown. He was trying to get the gun lined across the big trunk.

I whispered, "Shoot it in the ribs."

My own anguish was excruciating. It is vital that a youngster not "mess-up" on that first one. A miss is fine, but wounding can be traumatic and turn a kid off for good.

I realized I was holding my breath, and I also realized that Terry was on tip-toes. A heck of a way to shoot! He hadn't been taught that!

Then he whispered, "I can't see the ribs. All I can see is the head and some neck."

Of course! He was too short. I said, "Okay, shoot it in the neck."

I knew this was surely a blown chance. Our Hill Country does have necks about as big as a baseball bat. When the gun blast jarred my breath loose, the deer miraculously hit the turf without a quiver. With a whoop, Terry started to run. I hated to dull the fine edge of the greatest deer hunting jubilance and excitement he'd ever know, but I barked at him to stop. His amazed look would have melted me, but I couldn't afford sentiment.

"Did you reload?" I asked him.

He looked at the bolt of the rifle. "Gee, I dunno."

Purposely I let the pause run along and finally said, "Terry, you always must know. Excitement is never an excuse. Besides, when you shoot and a deer falls, you automatically reload before you even move — always. Suppose it gets up, and you're fumbling around? There's plenty of time to get a dead deer. Just make sure first that it is!"

Sheepishly he worked the bolt. I said, "And put the safety on. Excitement won't do as an excuse for ever forgetting that."

My boys were fortunate, growing up in Texas, where deer are abundant and each license allows several. We've long had our own place, so they could pack in an immense amount of experience. I presume Terry, for example, has killed to date more than 20 — Mike still more. However, the other side of the coin is that for an impressionable youngster, the very commonness of one after another can lead to lack of discrimination and respect.

So it was that after the last bite of Terry's first deer had been eaten, each meal duly pronounced the best venison we'd ever had, I said to him, "This season, maybe you can get two deer."

That second season, I laid out the ground rules. Terry was after a buck. After he'd taken one, if he got one, any deer would do for a second.

"How big a buck?" he asked apprehensively.

"Any buck, this time. Play 'em as they show. Maybe after this year, though, we'll hunt only eight-pointers."

Deciding to hunt a six-point or an eight-point or better and ending a season with the tag unfilled is the sort of discipline that separates the polished hunters from the bumblers. One is forced to learn his animals and their habits and to sharpen his craft to a fine edge in order to succeed.

We went through those lessons that fall. Terry's first kill that season was a so-so forkhorn. I said nothing as our six-week season progressed about what he had in mind for a second deer. But I noticed that he had chances at several does and passed them up. I knew then, and was pleased. He had caught the spark, sensed the satisfaction of hunting for something a little bit special, not just killing a deer.

For fun I said, deadpan, "We sure need to take some does off our place. Here I've got seven permits, and between you and Mike, so far no help."

"Maybe on the last day I'll help, if . . ."

"If what?"

"If I haven't got an eight by then."

As it turned out, he did get the eight. I was beginning to believe that I had another coming-along, authentic deer hunter.

Even at his tender age, Terry had seen me turn down shots because the stance of the deer or its movement didn't suit me. I recall how exasperated he was, watching me do this before he'd hunted. His third fall, I sharply forbade him to shoot at a certain standing buck because its rear was quartering toward us. Sure, an expertly placed bullet might range on a fine angle forward into the rib cage, but a slight slip might put it straight into the deer's paunch.

You don't have to shoot just because you see a deer. On an awesome trophy, a gamble might be taken, but surely not on an ordinary animal. You judge first if you believe you can make the shot good, an instant kill, or if there's too much chance of fouling things up.

Terry learned how to sit soundlessly, clearing a place for his feet so he didn't crash sticks, his back against cover. He learned how to walk in awesomely slow motion, always in shadow, always watching where his next footfall would come down and skirting instinctively the hardwood trees beneath which dry leaves would crackle. He also learned how to hunt with binoculars. He could actually sit for half an hour boring into the cover with the glasses.

I began more and more to turn Terry loose on his own. You might question whether I had really taught him all about deer hunting. In my view, I had imparted what is truly important. Techniques? Reading deer sign? Learning deer foods? Deer habits? While he was learning how to be the proper kind of deer hunter, all this had been seeping in.

You can't hunt selectively with success without learning the basic how-to. The fanatic emphasis for years has been on the routine without any emphasis on the correct philosophy of the sport. We turn out some efficient deer *killers* but not very many well-disciplined deer *hunters*.

Soon Terry was telling me discoveries he had made about deer habits that even I had failed to discover over my years of hunting. I made sure to let him know he was now teaching me. He had long ago given up trying to out-run or out-maneuver an alerted deer. He knew you might outwit their eyes and ears, but you could never play loose with air currents, hoping, as hunters so often do, that a deer won't wind you.

By his faintly whispered words or smallest gesture when we hunted together, I knew that he now knew the anathema, to a deer, of the human voice. Stoic patience also grew, along with the realization that a deer hunter has to learn to suffer gracefully when cold, cramped, or hungry.

The greatest part was when I realized we were just hunting together.

I wasn't giving advice. Sometimes he did, instead, planning sound strategy. Mike was no longer telling Terry what he ought to do.

There we were finally, on that 1977 mule deer hunt in West Texas. My thoughts of past times were still tumbling through my memory as I watched Terry atop the boulder, gun rested across the mashed-down crown of Jim Barbee's hat. The shot reverberated off the slopes and the rimrock. It was a bold punctuation point of sorts, denoting that there, atop the boulder, was the finished product I had so carefully nurtured from scratch.

For a second, neither Barbee nor Terry moved. Then Terry's right hand flashed swiftly, working the bolt, his eye still at the scope. I smiled. I was back there with that very first deer 13 years ago. Barbee arose. I saw Terry reach to pull back the safety. Without a word, they moved at a right angle toward the steep slope.

I watched, tailing them, as Jim followed Terry to the deer. I heard Barbee say, "Did we count right, Terry?"

Turning, grinning happily, Terry replied, "Yeah. It's a fine 10."

A moment later all of us were at the buck, all talking at once with the excitement only the hunter knows and cannot lucidly explain boiling inside us. I saw Barbee bend down, looking for the shot hole. Then he straightened, pulling out his knife as he did and laying on Terry a grin of total approval. He moved on around and clapped Terry on the shoulder.

"You were sure right," he said with a wide grin. "You do manage — just fine!"

CHAPTER 30
DEER! WHO NEEDS 'EM?

For many years I've hunted whitetails and loved every minute of it. For the past 30, I've lived with deer year-round. That relationship has been quite different. It has made my lifetime experience with these exasperating animals a love/hate combination.

We live near a small Hill Country, Texas, city, on 27 acres with two ponds. Around us subdivisions scar the hills. The deer of the area use our place as bedroom, dining room and playground. We're convinced that they believe *we're* the interlopers. We try to be neighborly. In winter my wife, Ellen, frets about their well-being, and runs up a corn bill that would make a roasted haunch of one of the critters worth a hundred bucks. What do we get in return? Here's an example:

Our yard covers 3½ acres. Scattered over it are yuccas, the variety that thrust bloom stalks 5 feet into the air. I've carefully mowed around scores of these plants for years. My wife loves the bell-shaped white blooms. But seldom do we get to see one. When the stalks are about 2 feet high, looking like giant asparagus, the deer select a specific night, and eat every one.

Within a few feet of the house is a patch of poor soil that is solid yuccas. Last spring there were 32 buds on them. My wife said the deer could have all the yuccas except those near the house. She had purchased a set of decorative camel bells, which she hung on a low oak limb above the yucca patch. For two nights they kept us awake — *jangle, jangle*.

"You see?" Ellen said each morning, "the yucca buds are still there."

The third night every bud over the entire yard was gone. I checked tracks under the jangling bells. I swear these looked as if the deer had been dancing while enjoying their nighttime yucca buffet.

Thousands of suburban households go through deer depredations. Whitetails are such determined colonizers that they now live in town and city environs almost everywhere in the nation. A friend of ours raises tomatoes — or tries to — on a large lot in town. Deer beat him to them. He built a "deer-proof" fence 7 feet tall. The night the fence was completed, the deer hurdled it, broke it down in places, and cleaned him out.

"Hang net bags of human hair along the fence and on your garden plants," a neighbor told him as he repaired the fence and replanted. "That's guaranteed to keep deer out."

It did — until his tomatoes were fat and red, and his okra pods were just right for picking. Then one night the deer made a raid. No more garden. That gentleman felt like I did about the yuccas. He said, "If they took a bite or two every few nights, I wouldn't be so mad. But they plan this: a special night to raid. It's downright insulting."

Ellen raises geraniums in pots each summer. Deer won't touch geraniums. I read it in a scientific report about deer depredations. Ellen sets the pots in a row on each side of the brick steps to our front porch. "You see," she told me happily the first year. "The deer don't like that smell." Later on, her geraniums bloomed, in varied shades of red and pink. She was delighted. One night when they were all at their best, we heard noises out front. Burglars? The noises subsided. We switched on the outdoor lights. What a clatter. The culprits fled, every flower and bud in their bellies.

A South Carolina friend who was having deer trouble in suburbia sent us a clipping about a cure. It was from a slick magazine for urban-country dwellers. Just sprinkle mothballs around your plants, it said. We tried this the next year on some tulips we'd planted near the front steps. I hate the smell of mothballs. I held my breath, going in and out. When the tulip buds came, Ellen really laid down the mothballs. The blooms opened amid the vile smell. A letter came from South Carolina: The mothballs didn't work. That night our own deer proved it. They got every bloom. What really riled me was that they didn't touch the leaves.

Watching deer, of course, has become a pastime of households everywhere, in both town and country. The animals, once almost extinct, caught on quickly that humans, growing all sorts of exotic as well as staple foods, actually made their lives better. Living was easier. What difference did towns make? People were so stupid they'd feed encroaching deer just to observe them.

Having watched deer around our place daily for 30 years, I often wonder why. That regal buck I picture in my hunter's mind comes timidly to the corn we put out in fall. Several old does rush the buck every time he tries for a mouthful. They run him clear out of the area. When he sneaks back, they chase him again. And, if the does come too close to one another, the oldest will rear up on its hind legs and flail the other. At times, both animals whack the bejabbers out of each other.

Watching a group of deer eating $4-per-bag corn is a ringside seat to incessant bickering and bullying. Even fawns of the year chop at each other. If one tries to nuzzle its mother, she strikes it. In summer when fawns are tiny, mostly twins, we watch a pair that wanders near a doe that isn't their mother. She gives them a crack on head or ribs with a sharp hoof. Sometimes their own mother, when eating our largesse as we watch, belts her fawns if they try to nurse her. The whole darned bunch are a petulant, crotchety gang of wild hoodlums.

I often think as I watch their actions: Deer! Who needs 'em? And as the years go on we realize that this oasis we own and live on among the subdivisions really isn't ours. The deer own it. They do whatever they please. We must adjust what we wish to do because of them.

There is, for example, the matter of the crape myrtle. As everyone knows, crape myrtle is a kind of symbol of the South. A friend from another state sent us a bulletin from some testing organization, saying deer will not eat crape myrtle. Ellen bought a crape myrtle shrub for a birthday present for me. Here at last was something we could grow. We nurtured it tenderly. It bloomed. Beautiful! And only a few feet from my large office window, so I could fully enjoy it. Deer won't eat crape myrtle, eh? They took the blooms first. What made me furious was that they waited until every bloom was fully opened. I'm absolutely convinced that they do this with everything we try to raise, just to irritate us more. After they'd eaten the flowers, they waited a bit, letting us hope more blooms would appear. Then one night they ate all the leaves and browsed most of the branches.

There are, of course, cures for all these deer depredations. We have a collection of them from throughout the South, clippings from newspapers and magazines, letters from friends. One recalls the days when women were prone to fainting spells, and "smelling salts" was carried for revival purposes. Ammonia was a main ingredient. Set saucers of ammonia near your plants or in your garden at night. This will drive the deer away. Sure. You bet.

We bought a large supply of ammonia when we planted a batch of amaryllis bulbs along our front walk. When the leaves were growing nicely, Ellen set the saucers along the walk. They looked silly. Friends who visited choked and gasped. We learned to walk swiftly out to the car, holding our breath. A nuisance, but by golly it worked. Buds showed. Their stalks grew. Ellen kept the saucers full. We were finally going to be able to grow something we wanted.

We began to sit on the porch each morning, looking at the buds. We wanted to see them actually open into their large red blooms. Of course, the process was too slow to watch, but one morning there were the beautiful flowers! Eureka! Ellen replenished the ammonia. For two mornings we sat and enjoyed the amaryllis. Later I imagined I could hear the deer saying, "OK, they think they've succeeded. Now let's show 'em." That night they not only ate every flower, but also everything else in sight — even the leaves of a small mesquite we'd been pampering. The ammonia, I decided, far from fending them off, had revved up their penchant for meanness.

I've pondered the immense popularity of deer hunting in the U.S.A., and believe I know why its appeal constantly increases: It's a matter of revenge.